Copyright © 2016 by Lani Sharp
All rights reserved. This book or any portion thereof
may not be reproduced or used in any manner whatsoever
without the express written permission of the publisher
except for the use of brief quotations in a book review.

Printed in Australia

First Printing, 2016

ISBN 978-0-9945051-8-7

White Light Publishing House
6 Lincoln Way
Melton West, VIC, Australia 3337

www.whitelightpublishingau.com

☙ DEDICATION ❧

When I was writing the dedication for each book in this series, I seemed to have no trouble finding a special person or people in my life to whom to dedicate each Sun sign. But when I got to the Aquarius, I realised I don't have any deeply affecting or personal friends or family who were born under this Sun sign. Therefore, at the suggestion of my other friends, I dedicate this book to two entities: The Aquarian kindred spirit who is yet to enter my life (I hereby ask the Universe for this), and in true Water Bearer fashion, I also dedicate these pages to the brotherhood and sisterhood that this sign represents. There is also a song which I believe sums up the collective archetypal Aquarian experience: 'He Ain't Heavy, He's My Brother'. I believe we are all connected as one and we are all here to carry each other. So thank you, my fellow Water Carriers, for your humane wisdom, application and knowing. Your very unique brand of special magic surely keeps our world spinning.

ABOUT THE AUTHOR

☾ ★ ☽

Lani Sharp is a Natural Born Rebel who just also happens to be an Aquarian, who shunned 'conventional' astrology courses to pursue her own path in the wondrous, inspiring and ever-evolving field of cosmic forces and stellar influences. After failing to find a course or tutor that suited her needs, Lani set out on her own starry Magic Carpet adventure across the skies, partly to discover her own 'truths' about this ancient system, but mostly to prove that one can achieve absolutely anything, including and above all, their dream careers (or lifestyle), if they put their hearts and souls into it. A self-taught astrologer who takes the esoteric and spiritual approach to this much-loved popular art, she has been studying and effectively practising astrology since she was eight years old. When she is not writing about, channelling, practising or teaching astrology, she can be found living her dream life alternating somewhere between her home in Australia's stunning Tropical North or her second home in Victoria's beautiful Dandenong Ranges, enjoying tea parties with her highly imaginative Cancerian daughter, Allira, and their gnome and fairy friends, crystal-wishing, day-dreaming, believing in gnomes, pixies, angels, fairies, magic and miracles, honing her magickal * witchcraft skills, Moon-gazing, Sun-worshipping, Venus-channelling, Jupiter-drawing, assisting others to discover, unravel and follow their true spiritual paths … or of course walking across rainbows!

Not a mistake. Magick is a Wiccan variation of the word 'magic'.

★

ACKNOWLEDGEMENTS, CREDITS & GRATITUDE BLESSINGS

I would love to thank the following people and entities for their amazing contributions, interest, support and faith in me as I wrote the manuscripts for each of the twelve astrological Sun signs. Firstly, the biggest thank you go to my Mum, Sandra, and my stepdad, Barry, for their unending support, love, advice, daily Skype conversations, acceptance of our geographical distance, and above all, their inner knowing that everything always comes together in the end. Your support of me and my dreams is appreciated beyond words. Secondly, gratitude to my wonderful partner, Travis, for his patience (no mean feat for a Gemini!), for supporting me every step of the way, and for his acceptance of my 'mad scientist' Aquarian mindset by never trying to break down the invisible 'laboratory' walls I built around myself while writing the books. I would also like to extend my enormous gratitude to the following: Allira, my little Cancerian 'crab' daughter, a soul in a billion, who also had to tolerate and operate within the bounds of her nutty professor mother's antics and focus throughout the writing of the books. Thank you to Nicola, my wonderful Facebook friend, for recommending White Light Publishing House, and of course to White Light Publishing House themselves, for pouring their faith and passion into my project from the very beginning - and an even bigger thank you to the wonderful people behind the company for publishing my work, Christie and Jess! Gratitude also goes out to my dear friends, both near and far, who have inspired in me so many ideas through simply being themselves - especially Amanda and Carlie. Amanda, you have always been my 'astrology buddy' and I have always enjoyed - and learned so much through - our discussions on all things astrology and star signs: the good, the bad and the ugly! Having someone like you off which to bounce thoughts and share ideas with, has always been immensely helpful and appreciated. I have saved my final thank you for The Universe, who always delivers to me exactly what I have asked for, without exception. The Universe is my ultimate *higher power*, my guiding light, my powerful driving force, my spiritual helper, my guardian angel, my eternal friend, my inner motivator, my sympathetic listener, my inspirational teacher, and the fulfiller of all my dreams, including this one, having my very first book(s) published, a long-held dream that stretches way back through the years to my days of being a mini dreamer, inquisitor and stargazer. The Universe has always believed in me, but perhaps more importantly, I have always believed in *IT*.

So to all of the above, I wish to say:

Thank you, thank you, thank you!

"We were born at a given moment, in a given place, and like vintage years of wine, we have the qualities of the year and of the season in which we are born"

Carl G. Jung

"There was a star danced,
and under that I was born"

William Shakespeare

INSPIRED BY ALL THE SIGNS

Aries imparted courage and boldness
And helped me dance away the pain
Taurus gave me hugs and comfort
And shelter from the rain
Gemini provided me with laughter
And taught me again how to have fun
Cancer nurtured and sustained me
By reflecting back my Sun
Leo reminded me there was joy
From within myself and above
Virgo awakened my healthy glow
By teaching me how to love
Libra gave me gentle hugs
And judged me not for a thing
Scorpio lent me some of his power
And took away the sting
Sagittarius showered me with gifts
Of words so wise and true
As Capricorn led the way up the mountain
My resolve and strength grew
Aquarius gave me the gift of friendship
And carried me as his brother
And Pisces swam with me to the depths
With a compassion like no other.

♒

"She's susceptible to sudden flashes of inspiration, and her intuition is remarkable. Her judgement may not seem sound or practical at first, because she sees months and years ahead. The Aquarian girl lives in tomorrow. What she says will come true, perhaps after many delays and troubles, but it will come true. I suppose, after all, that's the most special thing about your Aquarian woman. She's a little bit magic."

Linda Goodman

♒

Special Note

Throughout the text of this book, and indeed the whole Lucky Astrology book series, I have capitalised the first letter of the word 'Universe'. This is because, quite simply, I feel it is a very special title for the higher power that I personally choose to be guided by, and have accordingly highlighted it as such.

You may also notice that I use the words 'he' or 'she', and 'his' or 'her', when referring to your own Sun sign and other zodiac signs, and never 'he or she' or 'his or her' together. The reason for this is for simplicity, for I don't wish the sentences to be too wordy and therefore the messages within them to be lost. As a general rule, I refer to all six 'masculine' zodiac signs as 'he', and all six 'feminine' signs as 'she', and this remains a consistent rule throughout this book and the whole series.

Your Sun sign, Aquarius, is a masculine sign and will thus be referred to accordingly.

CONTENTS

	Page
ASTROLOGY	17
THE ZODIAC & YOUR PLACE IN THE SUN	26
AQUARIUS THE WATER BEARER	33
QUOTES BY AQUARIANS	39
THE AQUARIUS CONSTELLATION	43
THE AQUARIUS SYMBOL	45
THE RUNDOWN & LESSONS ★	
THE ESSENCE OF AQUARIUS	49
THE THREE DECANS OF AQUARIUS	66
YOUR ELEMENT ★ AIR	70
YOUR MODE ★ FIXED	92
YOUR RULING PLANET ★ URANUS	95
YOUR HOUSE IN THE HOROSCOPE ★	
THE ELEVENTH HOUSE	111
YOUR OPPOSITE SIGN ★ LEO	114
MAGIC, DRAWING, ATTRACTION, SPELLS, RITUALS, WISHING & POWER	121
ASTROLOGY & MAGIC	126
PLANETS ★ DAYS OF THE WEEK & THEIR POWERS	132
YOUR NATAL MOON PHASE	136
SPELLS, MAGIC & WISHING WITH MOON PHASES	139
THE MOON ★ WHAT T REPRESENTS IN THE HUMAN PSYCHE & NATAL CHART	146
YOUR MOON SIGN	149
YOUR BODY & HEALTH	157
THE CELL SALTS ★ ASTROLOGICAL TONICS	162

	Page
AIR SIGN AQUARIUS & THE SANGUINE HUMOUR	165
MONEY ATTRIBUTES	168
COLOURS ★ YOUR LUCKY COLOURS	172
LUCKY CAREER TIPS	184
LUCKY PLACES	188
GEMS & CRYSTALS	189
VIRGOAN POWER CRYSTALS	201
YOUR LUCKY NUMBERS	211
YOUR LUCKY MAGIC HOURS OR TIME UNITS	219
YOUR LUCKY DAY ★ SATURDAY	224
YOUR LUCKY CHARM / TALISMANS	228
YOUR LUCKY ANIMALS & BIRDS	231
YOUR METALS	242
PLANTS, HERBS, SPICES, TREES, SHRUBS, FLOWERS, SCENTS & INCENSE	246
YOUR FOODS	252
YOUR LUCKY WOOD & CELTIC TREE ★ PINE & BIRCH OR ROWAN	254
THE POWER OF LOVE	262
LUCKY IN LOVE? AQUARIUS COMPATIBILITY	274
YOUR TAROT CARDS	288
LUCKY 13 TIPS	309
HAVE YOU PACKED YOUR MAGICAL BAG FOR THE JOURNEY?	312
A FINAL WORD ★ TAPPING INTO THE MAGIC OF AQUARIUS	313

LUCKY ASTROLOGY

By Lani Sharp

AQUARIUS

*Tapping into the Powers of Your Sun Sign for Greater
Luck, Happiness, Health, Abundance & Love*

"That which is above is like to that which is below, and that which is below is like to that which is above, to accomplish the miracles of one thing ... the Father thereof is the Sun, the mother the Moon."

The Emerald Tablet, Hermes Trismegistus, (circa 3000 BC)

★ ASTROLOGY ★

Astrology: "Divination through the correlation of earthly events with celestial patterns"
'Real Magic', I. Bonewits, 1971

A BRIEF HISTORY

Astrology can be defined as the calculation and meaningful interpretation of the positions and motions of the heavenly bodies, and their correlation with human experiences. Its central concept is based upon this interconnectedness or correspondence between the stars and ourselves.

The word astrology is derived from the Greek word astron, meaning 'star' and logos which means 'word'. Astrology, therefore, literally means language of the stars. It is based on the ancient law known as 'As Above, So Below', otherwise known as the Law of the Macrocosm and Microcosm. The Macrocosm is the Universe, symbolised by the sky, the starry dome that we can see from the Earth; the Microcosm is us - humans, and all other life on Earth. 'As Above, So Below' is a well-known and deeply impressing maxim of Hermetic origin, inscribed upon the famed Emerald Tablet among cryptic wording by enigmatic figure, Hermes Trismegistus, around 5,000 years ago. These four powerful words are adopted by astrologers and believers in magic to explain, in very succinct wording, the meaning behind the art and science of celestial influences upon our Earthly affairs.

Astrology and many other magical and occult studies, propose that we are not separate from the Universe, we are part of it. The Sun, Moon and planets all follow exact patterns of movement and their motions can be measured precisely by astronomers. The basic idea of astrology is that all individual parts of the Universe, from plants to animals, cooperate with each other and work together in harmony.

Anyone can apply astrological knowledge in their daily lives, but it hasn't always been like that. At one time, astrology was reserved only for Kings and nations, and only the court astrologer/astronomer could cast and interpret horoscopes. Ancient astrology and astronomy used to be one and the same. To be an astrologer, you first had to be able to interpret the stars in some systematic way, and then track the movement of the Moon and the planets against the background of the constellations.

Astrology, the knowledge and language of the cosmos, goes back to the ancient kingdom of Babylonia and was adapted by the Mesopotamians, Greeks, Egyptians and Romans to incorporate their own deities (as indicated in mythology). It is upon a combination of Greek and Egyptian interpretations of astrology that our present knowledge is based.

In the ancient Mesopotamian world, as far back as 800 BC, people lived precariously beneath the open skies. The skies and the stars which filled them, were the real founders of astrology. Today we are aware that the Sun and Moon exert a profound influence upon our Earthly affairs, but for our primitive ancestors, the heavens, the stars and the planets must have been a matter of great and mysterious significance. Early humankind, its senses influenced by natural processes of ebbs, flows, growth, decay and cycles, tended naturally towards a physical explanation of the Universe. At first, the movements of the planets - and all celestial occurrences - were observed as omens affecting the Ruler and his nation; it was only in Egypt in the fifth century AD that the casting of horoscopes for individual people and the calculation of the planetary positions at the time of birth became widespread.

The first astrologers, the Chaldeans, mapped the stars and later passed this knowledge and wisdom on to the ancient Greeks, who, during the third century BC, developed astrology into a science with the use of mathematical aids and instruments to measure planetary movements. The Greeks were the first to cast individual horoscopes. And it was the Greeks who associated the four elements with the signs of the zodiac. The word "zodiac" can be translated from Greek to mean the "circle or path of the animals." The Greeks not only had names for the twelve Solar phases but had symbols for each, and many correspond with the ones we use today.

The Greeks passed on much of their knowledge to the Romans. During the second century BC, Roman astrologers were primarily forecasters who were consulted frequently by rulers of the church and state. By the early third century AD, astrology co-existed with early Christianity. This harmonious co-existence was possible because it was considered that celestial bodies could foretell events, but did not determine the future - indeed, the stars seen by the shepherds at the time of Christ's birth were only predictors of his arrival. After the fourth century AD, Christianity strengthened and the popularity of astrology declined as Christian reluctance to support 'pagan' or 'superstitious' beliefs became more prominent. The Middle Ages saw a revival in astrology, with courses being taught in universities and other educational establishments, and connections were made between the zodiac, alchemy, herbs and medicine. Astrology was once again able to exist alongside the Church, although many remained suspicious of astrologers.

Around the beginning of the fifteenth century, academics of the Renaissance movement examined the past for knowledge, and ancient philosophies, including astrology, flourished; this coincided with arts and science movements developing. The famous prophet and astrologer Nostradamus lived during this period. Leonardo da Vinci depicted aspects of astrology combined with geometry in his art. Writers and poets of the time, including Shakespeare, alluded to zodiacal influences in their work.

During this period, astrology had numerous practical applications. Agricultural calendars were introduced, indicating favourable planting times according to the phases of the Moon; health and illness were linked with movements of celestial bodies; and emotional states and mental health afflictions correlated with the planetary positions.

Eventually, new ways of thinking led to a split between astronomy and astrology, and by the seventeenth century, the realm of science had developed to such a degree that astrology was no longer taken seriously.

The study of the sky above us has been charted for more than 5,000 years. This fact is known because ancient 'horoscopes' imprinted on clay tablets have been unearthed, dating back almost 5,400 years ago. However, no one knows for certain just how, when and where astrology first began, although it is known that it flourished in ancient Chaldea, Mesopotamia, Babylon and Egypt.

Astrology is a science which has spanned many centuries and still remains extraordinarily popular, and its truths have the potential to speak to and *through* all of us. Long before today's interest in it, men of great vision such as Ptolemy, Hippocrates, Plato, Galileo, Jefferson, Franklin, Newton, Columbus and Jung respected its inherent truths, mythology and eternal knowledge. Furthermore, astrology predates many other 'sciences' - for out of it grew religion, medicine and astronomy, not the other way around.

The discipline of astrology is ultimately a study of the interlocking and interrelated forces of the twelve zodiacal forces, or constellations, that grace the heavens, as they pour their energies into the Earthly kingdoms below. As these various energies circulate throughout the etheric realm of our Solar system, these zodiacal entities and archetypes imprint their vibrational frequencies and harmonic resonances upon our bodies, minds, souls and spirits.

ASTROLOGY & THE INDIVIDUAL

Since the earliest period of the history of humankind, people studied the starry vaults of the heavens and conceived that their presence, movements and positions endowed planet Earth's inhabitants with divine influence. There is much evidence that positions and movements of the planets as seen from Earth at the time of a birth are linked to personality characteristics of individuals. Human energy and emotional cycles are governed by the forces and networks of magnetic impulses from all the planets. Of all the heavenly bodies, the Moon's effects and power are the most marked and visible due to its close proximity to Earth. But the Sun, Venus, Mars, Mercury, Jupiter, Saturn, Uranus, Neptune and Pluto exercise their influences just as surely. In fact, scientists are aware that plants and animals are affected by natural cycles which are governed by forces such as fluctuations in barometric pressure, the gravitational field and electricity in the air. These Earthly dynamics are originally triggered by magnetic vibrations from the atmosphere, or outer space, from where the planets send forth their unseen waves. No living organism or mineral on Earth escapes these immense, if unseen, influences.

The geomagnetic field seems to affect life on Earth in certain observed ways, and these influences appear to correlate with planetary positions. It has been suggested that the fluctuations of the Earth's magnetic field are picked up by the nervous system of the in utero infant, which acts like an antenna, and these synchronise the internal biological clocks of the foetus which control the moment of birth. The foetal magnetic antenna therefore, is sensitive enough to sense these planetary vibrations and fields, and through a combination of inherited genetics and the positions of the planets at birth, they are imprinted with certain basic inherited and 'absorbed' personality characteristics.

Carl Jung, the Swiss psychiatrist and psychological theorist, suggested that the inherent disposition of the individual is present at birth, and is reflected in the patterns of his or her natal chart. Further, he theorised that there is a 'priori factor' in all human activities, namely the inborn, preconscious and unconscious individual structure of the psyche. The preconscious psyche, for example that of a newborn baby, is not simply an empty vessel into which practically anything can be poured, but rather it is this preconscious psyche that gives us the free will to become what we are instead of what others or our environment makes us. The child is not merely a receptacle for the psychic life of those around him or her, albeit sensitive and susceptible to the surrounding unconscious forces in childhood; for he/she also brings something of his own to his experience of them.

Further, Dr Harold S. Burr, who was a Professor of Anatomy at the Yale University School of Medicine, and author of *The Nature of Man and the Meaning of Existence* (1962), asserted that there is order in the Universe, unity in the organism and man is endowed with a soul. He stated that a complex magnetic field not only establishes the pattern of the human brain at birth, but continues to regulate and control it through life, and that the human central nervous system is a superb receptor of electro-magnetic energies, indeed the finest in nature. He contended that the electro-dynamic fields of all living things, which may be measured and mapped with standard voltmeters, mould and control each organism's development, health and mood, and named these fields 'fields of life'.

It can therefore be suggested that astrological and planetary influences endow us with the majority of our characteristics at birth, characteristics bestowed upon us according to our Sun sign and other planetary forces. Other parts of the chart are also highly significant and need to be integrated for a 'whole' picture to form, however the Sun sign is an excellent starting point.

The ancients taught that astrology was one of the keys to the many enigmas that plague humans in their unceasing quest to determine what the meaning of life is, and what their role and place in the Universe is - and this quest still persists today. Astrology, which dates back over 5,000 years, is indeed one such key to unlocking the many secrets of the Universe - and ultimately, the individual self.

"KNOW THYSELF"

Man, know thyself. All wisdom centres on this.
Carl Jung

Before the temple of the Oracle at Delphi, the ancient Greeks imparted a special piece of advice that was carved onto one of the portals: "Know Thyself." These two powerful words are easy enough to understand, but much more difficult to apply. Throughout life's inner and outer journey, astrology can provide us with an inner navigational system by which we can be guided towards our highest potential, and closer towards the eternal quest of 'knowing thyself'. It provides the hope that this higher spiritual plane exists and that if we can 'read' and therefore be guided by the unique inner blueprint that our individual birth chart has stamped upon us at the moment we take our very first breath, indeed we can reach this higher spiritual plane and realise our innate potential.

Always remember that astrology is not fatalistic. The stars may incline, but they do not compel. Astrology simply provides us with an inner guide, a blueprint, for our journey through life and the finding of our true selves - and what we do with the resulting knowledge is entirely up to us.

Good luck on your journey!

THE ZODIAC & YOUR PLACE IN THE SUN

The zodiac is a circle of 360 degrees, consisting of equal segments of 30 degrees each. These represent the twelve houses of the twelve astrological signs. This zodiac is how the early astrologers imagined the Solar system to be, a perfect circle with the Earth at its centre, around which the Sun, Moon and the planets revolved. Each sign of the zodiac corresponds to one of the twelve segments, following a chronological order and established according to the rhythm of the seasons and cycles of the Sun and the Moon. But the zodiac itself, or the band of constellations which comprise it, has shifted over the millennia, creating division between astronomical and astrological schools of thought. It has been said that due to this shift over time, one who once considered themselves as an Aquarian, is actually a Capricorn, the sign before it, and a Leo is actually a Cancerian, its preceding sign. This is the result of misunderstandings and differences in perspectives, and explanations around it are beyond the scope of this book, but can be researched further should you wish to delve a little deeper. From the astronomical point of view, it is true that the zodiac to which we refer today is not situated where it 'should' be, but indeed, nothing is fixed under the celestial vault. And so the starting point of the ancient zodiac does not correspond exactly to the one we can observe today. But for the purposes of increasing your power and luck, let's keep things simple and enjoy the ride; after all, astrology - while based upon many scientific theories, mysteries, scepticism, superstitions, facts, measurable patterns, ambiguities, correlations, paradoxes, contradictions, links, stigmatisms and observations that seek to support, refute, prove and disprove this ancient art time and again - is ultimately meant to be *fun* too!

THE SUN

Earth's Luminary ★ *Our Brightest Shining Star*

Our Centre, Core Self, Identity & Inner Guiding Light

"Perfect is what I have said of the work of the Sun."
Hermes Trismegistus, *The Emerald Tablet*

The Sun is our essence, centre, source, ego strength, power, life force, will, vitality, creative expression, purpose, life's direction, our sense of identity, and who we really *are*. Our brightest star is the core of our individuality, our inner guiding light. The Sun is externalising, and represents totality, infinity, eternity, the striving toward and ultimate reaching of one's personal destiny, and *completion* in all areas. It is the creative energising giver of life and the 'father' of the zodiac. It endows us with our inherent creative potential and personal identity - our urge to *create* and to *be*. The Sun is our core self, conscious purpose, our sense of creating something out of our own being. It is the integrated personality and represents the *present*, our greatest Gift. The Sun rules the heart and is thus symbolically the centre of self. Indeed, the Sun *is* the heart and the most commanding presence in our birth chart; the luminary Ruler who governs our essential self and wants to be noticed and appreciated, and above all, to *shine*.

★ KEY WORDS ★

Identity, core self, spirit, life force, power, essence, creativity, higher self, the Father, ego, vitality, pride, individuality, leadership, majesty, inner authority, will, expression, willpower, purpose, the journey, the path and the destiny.

THE SUN ★ THE ULTIMATE SOURCE OF LIFE ON EARTH

Throughout the ages, and indeed since life forms began, the electromagnetic waves generated by the Sun have kept planet Earth habitable for humans, animals, plants and minerals. The Sun is, in fact, the only true source of energy on planet Earth. It provides the perfect amount of energy for plants to synthesise all of the products required for growth and reproduction, which is then stored by plants and ingested by humans and animals who, through many complex processes, utilise these various forms of encapsulated Solar energy - and so the cycle continues. Wood, fuel and minerals (crystals included), too, are merely various forms of this encased Sun energy. In fact, all matter is essentially 'frozen' light. Human body cells are bundles of Sun energy; we couldn't conceive or process a single thought without the molecules of Solar-energised oxygen and glucose.

In essence, the Sun supports the growth of all species, including human beings and microscopic life forms, and without it life on Earth would simply not be possible. The mathematical and metaphysical complexity that stands behind a system of organisation and order so infinitely diverse and intricate as planetary life cannot be truly fathomed, but unerringly and miraculously, the Sun instinctively knows what each species, from a tree to a human, intrinsically needs in order to fulfil its evolutionary purpose and cycles.

Ultimately, the electromagnetic waves generated by the Sun come in a variety of lengths, which determine their specific course of action and responsibility. There are gamma rays, x-rays, cosmic rays, various kinds of ultraviolet rays, infrared, short-wave infrared, radio waves, electric waves, and of course the visible light spectrum, consisting of the seven colour rays.

Most of these energy waves are absorbed and used for various processes in the layers of atmosphere that encircle the Earth, and only a small portion of them - the electromagnetic spectrum - reach the surface of our planet. Although the human eye is only able to perceive about one percent of this spectrum, the waves exert a very strong influence upon us. The waves and rays which do affect us so profoundly, allow all life forms to undergo constant cycles of change necessary for growth and renewal. Physically, we can observe this, but on a deeper, more spiritual plane, we can even *feel* it and allow its radiance to permeate our very souls. Such is the might, force and power of that astonishing ball of fire in our sky: the brilliant, ever-shining Sun.

THE SUN ★ WHAT IT REPRESENTS IN THE HUMAN PSYCHE & NATAL CHART

☼

"The Sun is the most powerful of all the stellar bodies. It colours the personality so strongly that an amazingly accurate picture can be given of the individual who was born when it was exercising its power through the known and predicable influences of a certain astrological sign; these electromagnetic vibrations will continue to stamp that person with the characteristics of their Sun sign as they go through life."
Linda Goodman's Sun Signs, **Linda Goodman, Pan Books, 1968**

The Sun is our essence, our core self, conscious purpose and sense of identity, our creative potential, our spirit, the integrated personality that shines outward from within us. It is concerned with the present. It is our centre, source, power, life force, will, vitality, purpose, life's direction, what and who we *really* are.

The Sun represents our basic urge for self-expression. It is the 'Solar energy cell' in a person's character, the Lord and giver of life, and symbolises the way in which an individual will shine out to the world. Our Sun is our personal identity and aspects to it from other components in the chart show the ease or otherwise of assuredness and confidence with which one will project and express one's individuality. The Sun sign will also show how an individual bounces back from setbacks and disappointments, their resilience and their general outward expression of energy.

The Sun is the archetype of the Father and represents the primary masculine principle in the natal chart. It indicates how we express and experience our masculine side, or animus, our conscious self, how we express ourselves creatively, our personal potential, individuality, self-expression and personal power. It has to do with courage, power, generosity, creativity, vitality, self-confidence, nobility, self-worth, dignity and strength of will. It symbolises authority and purpose, the *ruler*, and its potential is the peak of constructive maturity. It signifies self-sufficiency and abundance, containing enough energy to radiate warmth and give life to everything around it.

The sign in which one's Sun is posited, and its placement in the birth chart, strongly indicates the level and type of vitality available to the personality (the sign), and in which area of life this may be most strongly directed (the house).

The Sun in a natal chart is a powerful symbol because everything is filtered, at a conscious level, through it. It tells us what we need to do to feel fully alive, the type of engine 'driving' us, what we need to do to be authentic and to be fully functioning. Listening to the special message of one's Sun sign can provide one with greater direction, and a more dynamic energy and life purpose.

The symbol for the Sun ☉ depicts a circle with a dot or 'seed' at its centre, from which the core self, power, creativity and the first sparks of life can spring. The circle around this 'seed' represents spirit, symbolising wholeness, eternity and the never-ending flow of energy.

While the Moon, the night sky's luminary, represents the *soul*, the Sun, the day sky's luminary, represents our *spirit*.

There is a reason your Sun sign is otherwise known as your Star Sign - it's because, quite simply, the Sun *is* a star; in fact, it's the largest, brightest, shiniest one in Earth's known visible Universe. This book is about your Sun sign and how you can become much larger, glow with far more brilliance, and shine brighter than you ever dreamed possible. I wish you all the magic in the galaxy for your dreams to come true and your deepest wishes to become reality, through tapping into the amazing power and inherent potential of your Sun sign. So get set for a galactical ride through the lucky stars of your constellation - and may a shooting star cross the path in front of you as you go!

AQUARIUS THE WATER BEARER

★ Fixed Air, Masculine, Positive, Thinking ★

"I pour the waters of knowledge forth onto a thirsty world"

Body & Health
Calves, ankles, circulation, spinal cord, nervous system

How Aquarius Emanates its Life Force / Energy
Originally, Objectively, Unconventionally, Gregariously

Is Concerned With
★ Experimentation ★ Scientific Thinking ★
★ Friendship ★ Brotherhood ★ Humanity ★
★ Kindness ★ Humaneness ★ Originality ★
★ Mystery, Intrigues, Enigmas ★ Magic ★ Genius ★
★ Eccentricity ★ Independence ★ Freedom ★
★ Politics ★ Creative Arts ★ Detachment ★
★ Electricity ★ Magnetism ★ Idealism ★ Logic ★
★ Telecommunications ★ Intellect ★ Rationality ★

Spiritual Aquarius

Your Archetypal Universal Qualities
The Humanitarian, Rebel, Reformer, Global One

What You Refuse
To be a follower, ordinary or conventional

What You Are an Authority On
Truth, Originality, Genius and Futuristic Thinking

The Main Senses Through Which You Experience Your Reality
Truth, Freedom, Independence, Originality

How You Love
Loyally, Detachedly, with Friendship

Positive Characteristics
★ Communicative ★ Thoughtful ★ Humane ★
★ Independence in Thought and Action ★
★ Inventive, Innovative ★ Unorthodox ★
★ Friendly ★ Intellectual ★ Faithful ★
★ Interested in Others ★ Cooperative ★
★ Absence of Ego and Arrogance ★ Loyal ★
★ Scientific ★ Unique ★ Original ★ Humane ★
★ Forward-thinking and Futuristic ★

Negative Characteristics
★ Unwilling to Share Ideas ★ Indolent ★
★ Erratic ★ Tactless ★ Rebellious ★
★ Eccentric ★ Perverse ★ Opinionated ★
★ Unwilling to Fight for Beliefs ★ Contradictory ★
★ Cranky ★ Aloof ★ Distant ★ Contrary ★
★ Afraid of Intimacy ★ Unpredictable ★
★ Voyeuristic Curiosity About People ★
★ Uncertainty ★ Lack of Confidence ★

To Bring Out Your Best

Travel to offbeat places and immerse yourself in different cultures; study foreign languages and diverse subjects; share your scientific, genius, insightful thinking with others; buy and use high-tech gadgets; be your own boss; express your individuality and shine!

Spiritual Goals

To shine brighter by unleashing your talents. To learn to commit and see that it ultimately leads to freedom. To be more discriminate in your social crusading and 'battles'. To develop greater self-confidence.

> *When the Moon is in the Seventh House*
> *And Jupiter Aligns with Mars*
> *Then peace shall guide the planets*
> *And love will steal the stars.*
> *This is the dawning of the Age of Aquarius.*
> **Aquarius, from the musical *Hair***

AQUARIUS

20 January - 18 February

Fixed Air

Ruled by Uranus

"I KNOW"

Gemstones ◊ Amethyst, Garnet, Aquamarine

★ Detached, independent, tolerant, innovative, social, people-oriented, honest, impersonal, eccentric, rebellious, reforming, liberal, democratic, altruistic, unconventional, erratic, distant, paradoxical, original, unpredictable, idealistic, friendly, futuristic, progressive, perverse, intellectual, contrary, quick, aloof, visionary, bohemian, experimental, New Age, mental, unorthodox, intuitive, brilliant, electric, scientific, different, quirky, egalitarian, self-willed, unstable, cool-headed, rational, unique ★

"'But I don't want to go among mad people,' Alice remarked. 'Oh, you can't help that', said the Cat. 'We're all mad here'" - *Alice in Wonderland*
Lewis Carroll

AQUARIUS

♒

★ Original ★ Free-spirited ★ Idealistic ★
★ Inventive ★ Independent ★ Eccentric ★
★ Visionary ★ Humanitarian

Aquarius is the sign of the Water Bearer, a man who pours the water of knowledge from its urn to benefit all of mankind. Friendly, inventive, detached, future-oriented, unconventional, rebellious, eccentric, aloof, idealistic and humanitarian are Aquarius's most notable traits. Being an intellectual air sign, this is a thinking rather than feeling character, and possesses a scientific and forward-thinking mind which it often puts to use for the advantage of all to great effect. Group-oriented but impersonal, Aquarius is often hard to pin down due to its aloof, cool and contrary nature. The Water Bearer is a paradoxical sign, with a great love of humankind but an aversion to close personal relationships; it is also broad-minded and far-sighted but tends to hide its intuitive truths and prophecies (which almost always come true) under a veil of contradiction, and perversely rebelling for its own sake. Humanitarian and social causes are a big thing for the progressive Water Bearer's spirit, and it will always fight for the underdog and those it feels are treated unfairly. Aquarius is futuristic, unorthodox, honest and truth-seeking, with very little ego but much conviction invested in its many ideals. An independent lover, loyal friend and with a great need for personal freedom, Aquarius is the eleventh sign and the offbeat and rebellious social crusader of the zodiac, whose lack of personal warmth is more than made up for by its gregarious far-reaching nature, and charitable and inventive contributions to all its fellow terrestrial inhabitants.

KEY CONCEPTS

★ Loyalty to a cause, ideal or idea ★
★ Talkative, active mentality ★
★ Gregarious, humane and sociable ★
★ Intuitive and alert mind ★
★ Impersonal, cool, aloof ★
★ Lacks sympathy on an individual or personal level ★
★ Zealous and fanatical ★
★ Conceives zany, impractical schemes ★
★ Strives for brotherhood ★
★ Can embrace and love all equally ★

SOME CORRESPONDENCES THAT ARE ASSOCIATED WITH AQUARIUS

Astrology, advanced thought, batteries, radio and television broadcasting, computers, reformers, researchers, cooperative societies, friendship clubs, altruism, hopes and wishes, invention, lightning, modern technology, nuclear physics, electricity, electronics, the new age, aeronautics, rebels, the space age, social circles, group activities, scientists, X-ray technicians, as well as anything which is Avant garde, detachment, erratic, unorthodox, nonconformist, unusual, quirky, rebellious, paradoxical and unpredictable. Take your pick and enjoy the ride!

QUOTES BY AQUARIANS

"To believe in the things you can see and touch is no belief at all; but to believe in the unseen is a triumph and a blessing" - Abraham Lincoln (12 February 1809)

"It's a funny thing about life; if you refuse to accept anything but the best, you very often get it" - W. Somerset Maugham (25 January 1874)

"Accomplishments have no colour" - Leontyne Price (10 February 1927)

"Genius is only one per cent inspiration and ninety-nine per cent perspiration" - Thomas Alva Edison (11 February 1847)

"A wise man will make more opportunities than he finds" - Francis Bacon (22 January 1561)

"I do not think much of a man who is not wiser today than he was yesterday" - Abraham Lincoln

"Good girls go to heaven, bad girls go everywhere" - Helen Gurley Brown (18 February 1922)

"There are only two ways of spreading light; to be the candle or the mirror that reflects it" - Edith Wharton (24 January 1862)

"It is not the strongest of the species that survive, nor the most intelligent, but the one most responsive to change" - Charles Darwin (12 February 1809)

"In charity there is no excess" - Francis Bacon

"A loving heart is the truest wisdom" - Charles Dickens (7 February 1812)

"It has been my experience that folks who have no vices have very few virtues" - Abraham Lincoln

"All men of action are dreamers" - James G. Huneker (31 January 1857)

"No one is useless in this world who eases the burden of it to anyone else" - Charles Dickens

"A person is not old until regret takes the place of dreams" - John Barrymore (15 February 1882)

"When you reach the end of your rope, tie a knot in it and hang on" - Franklin D. Roosevelt (30 January 1882)

"If I have eight hours to chop a tree, I spend six hours sharpening my axe" - Abraham Lincoln

"Truth is, everyone is going to hurt you. You just got to find the ones worth suffering for" - Bob Marley (6 February 1945)

"The great pleasure in life is doing what people say you cannot do" - Walter Bagehot (3 February 1826)

"Charity begins at home, and justice begins next door" - Charles Dickens

"In wilderness I sense the miracle of life, and behind it our scientific accomplishments fade to trivia" - Charles Lindbergh (4 February 1902)

"Every moment of one's existence is growing into more or retreating into less. One is always living a little more or dying a little bit" - Norman Mailer (31 January 1923)

"Real freedom lies in wildness, not in civilisation" - Charles Lindbergh

"Men are not prisoners of fate, but only prisoners of their own minds" - Franklin D. Roosevelt

"When I look into the future, it's so bright it burns my eyes" - Oprah Winfrey (29 January 1954)

"Life is like a landscape. You live in the midst of it but can describe it only from the vantage point of distance" - Charles Lindbergh

"Whatever you are, be a good one" - Abraham Lincoln

"Is it worse to be scared than to be bored, that is the question" - Gertrude Stein (3 February 1874)

"The height of your accomplishment will equal the depth of your convictions" - Walter Bagehot

"I try to decorate my imagination as much as I can" - Franz Schubert (31 January 1797)

"Man knows much more than he understands" - Alfred Adler (7 Feb 1870)

"Considering how dangerous everything is, nothing is really very frightening" - Gertrude Stein

"Your silence will not protect you" - Audre Lorde (18 Feb 1934)

"The only thing we have to fear is fear itself" - Franklin D. Roosevelt

"I've been rich and I've been poor. It's better to be rich" - Gertrude Stein

"You cannot teach a man anything; you can only teach him to discover it within himself" - Galileo Galilei (15 February 1564)

"The biggest adventure you can take is to live the life of your dreams" - Oprah Winfrey

THE AQUARIUS CONSTELLATION

The signs of the zodiac are the twelve symbolic features that ancient people imagined while observing the heavens. They saw shapes, patterns, faces, and natural and supernatural beings in the stars, from which they established, over centuries, a kind of celestial hierarchy and system based upon their observations. Groupings of stars became constellations, and twelve of these constellations make up the zodiac, a Greek word meaning 'circle of animals', that we know today.

Star constellations are not really self-contained groups but are particularly bright stars that give the appearance of being close together and form distinctive patterns. These are the patterns that over the ages have been identified as animals, deities or mythological figures and heroes. The stars are the living past. We receive their light long after it has left the star itself and so they are a good focus for escaping from the parameters of time. Their stellar influence is analogous with the aura, the bio/psychic energy field surrounding humans, animals, plants, crystals and even places. These individual energy systems interact with the energy waves emanated by other people, and even the cosmic rays emitted by planetary bodies, for psychic energies are not limited by time or distance.

The cluster of stars we know as Aquarius the Water Bearer, is, like Capricorn, a large, faint and unremarkable constellation, and its shape is hard to relate to its name, although it has been said to be in a vague shape of a water urn. It is likely that its name was derived from ancient times when heavy rains and floods tended to occur in the Northern Hemisphere when the Sun was located in this sign.

WISHING UPON YOUR STAR

The practice of wishing upon a star is familiar to most of us, and is a mystical superstition that is ingrained in many of us from childhood. As a night-time ritual, you can wish upon your own sign's constellation or that of the sign whose energies you wish to call forth; indeed, you can wish upon any constellation you feel an affinity with. If you can't see a particular constellation in your night sky, you can always meditate on it in your mind, or you can use the traditional technique of wishing upon the first star you see, while reciting the popular rhyme: *Star light, star bright, first star I see tonight, I wish I may, I wish I might, have the wish I make this night!* Any one of the three rituals will hold power for your own special wish. Good luck!

THE AQUARIAN SYMBOL ♒

Astrology uses symbols or 'glyphs' to represent the planets and signs. The glyph is made up of shapes representing the energy and physical matter of which the Universe is composed, and how these shapes are used in each symbol provide hints as to the properties of the sign or planet it represents.

The ancient view was that there were five elements: Fire, Water, Air, Earth and Ether (or Spirit). Ether is invisible energy, while the four tangible elements are known as 'matter'. Ether, as pure energy, cannot be influenced by any of the physical/matter elements, although it surrounds them and indeed fuels them. The Greek philosopher and scientist Aristotle regarded this idea as a circle (Ether/Spirit) with a cross (matter) in the centre. This glyph is used in astrology as a symbol for Earth, and the cycle of life. All the symbols used in astrology represent the relationship between energy and the 'matter' elements.

The image of Aquarius is that of a Water Bearer pouring forth the waters of knowledge and consciousness onto humanity. However, these flowing waters are often mistakenly linked with the Water element, leading many to consider Aquarius a Water sign, when it is in fact an Air sign. Furthermore, the glyph for Aquarius is two waves, one on top of the other, and this was the Egyptian hieroglyphic for water. With all the obvious references to liquid ('Aquarius' itself was derived from the Latin aqua = water), it is little wonder that Aquarius is often mistaken for a Water sign.

The meaning of Aquarius is intertwined with the concept of a divine substance which nourishes all life, this substance being variously described as the waters of life, or a life-giving liquid. The esoteric significance of its meaning and symbol relates to the fluids that the Man in the image distributes from his urn, in that they are actually the waters of consciousness, or knowledge, which are related to the mind (the Air element) that he is pouring from his vessel, and not related to 'pouring forth' of feelings or emotions (the Water element). This consciousness embraces the concept that all humans are brothers, a concept which can only be felt intuitively, and it is this powerfully intuitive aspect of mind that is embodied by the intellectually-based Air sign of Aquarius.

The Aquarian mind can use these communicative and rational faculties to broadcast the message of oneness and brotherhood to others, through such media as speech and writing. The water from his urn is alive and swarming with ideas that can be beneficially useful for humanity. One modern interpretation is that as Aquarius rules electricity, then its glyph should be interpreted as electrical waves rather than as liquid.

The glyph does not represent a still pool, it depicts waves rippling over water, and it is the winds, or air, which cause the waves to ripple; the Aquarian symbol is therefore suggestive of air currents creating the motion, indicating that Aquarius is indeed a sign of Air and movement, the 'mover' and disseminator of knowledge, the teacher, the inspirational visionary.

Being strongly connected with communication, electrical charges and the transmission of information through the activity of brain waves, for example, it seems valid that the Aquarian symbol represents all communication functioning through air currents and electrical impulses - again, symbolised by the two waves.

A further meaning can be derived from the fact that the urn is facing downwards, towards the Earth, indicating that knowledge exists on the heavenly plane and must be transmitted to Earthlings - and this is the wavelength to which most Aquarians resonate. The Water Bearer's urn and the enlightenment it dispenses, has a strong link with the Aquarian mind, and those Aquarians who are not properly in touch with this concept, or who have presented it to a world which is not quite ready to receive it, can find themselves in a lonely, isolated place. Such feelings of loneliness can lead to feeling out of harmony with 'Earthly realms', and a despondent Aquarian will quickly learn how desolate it can be at the top of the proverbial mountain.

THE AGE OF AQUARIUS ★ 2000 - 4000 AD

The beginning of the Age of Aquarius heralds a gentler, rational and more peaceful time for the human race. Throughout the 20th century and into the 21st, we have been on the cusp of two astrological eras: the end of the Age of Pisces, and the beginning of the Age of Aquarius. This change can be seen clearly in the way that history and society are coming under the influence of the intellectual, outward-looking, futuristic, humanitarian, global-minded Aquarius. Psychology, rationalism and science have largely replaced religion as our way of explaining and indeed experiencing our world; religious and spiritual powers have, to a large degree, lost ground to secular government. The revolution of mass production, the global use of electricity and power, telephones, television, social media and the Internet is glaringly apparent and can be directly attributed to Aquarius, the sign that regulates the flow of electricity, innovation, progress, globalisation, futuristic thinking and technology. The egalitarian quality of Aquarius is also reflected in the changing social climate - more pervasive democratic systems, better awareness of equal rights and greater racial cohesion are examples. Aquarius is the sign of foresight, and this is illustrated by the rise of ecological and environmental movements. People are now considering the long-term effects of humanity's actions and we are seeking to make changes that will enable our planet and its people to survive well into the future.

THE RUNDOWN & LESSONS
SOME QUIRKS, ODDITIES, UNIQUE CHARACTERISTICS AND IDIOSYNCRASIES OF AQUARIUS

"Lots of people like rainbows. Children makes wishes on them, artists paint them, dreamers chase them, but the Aquarian is ahead of everybody.
He lives on one …"
Linda Goodman

"At least I knew who I was when I got up this morning, but I think I must have changed several times since then."
Alice's Adventures in Wonderland, **Lewis Carroll**

There are two types of thinkers: what I like to call 'right-brainers' and 'left-brainers'. The left hemisphere of the human brain deals with things such as control of speech, verbal functions, reason, logic, mathematics, linear concepts, details, sequences, the intellect and analysis; the right hemisphere is concerned with spatial, music, holistic, artistic concepts, as well as simultaneity and intuition. You could go on to say that the left brain is masculine or yang in quality, and the right brain is feminine or yin in quality. Based upon these very simplistic outlines, it can be further stated that Air sign Aquarius dwells mainly in the left hemisphere, with a bit of right thrown in for good measure.

The cerebral nature of Air highlights thought rather than emotion and feeling. Aquarius is largely motivated by reasoning processes. Positive, hot, moist, sanguine and rational, a determined (Fixed) intellectual (Air) approach characterises the sign of Aquarius.

Aquarius is the last of the airy signs, is positive in magnetism, and is ruled by the mighty planets Saturn and Uranus. People born under this sign are generally idealistic, generous and humane, and are quick to relieve the distress or wants of others. Shrewd and intelligent characters, they are acutely sensitive to outside impressions, and are blessed with a natural gift for sensing the magnetic auras of any people or places with which they come into contact. Strong champions of progress in every direction, they long to sweep away that which is corrupt or burdensome and replace it with something more serviceable to the welfare of humanity.

Your instinctive behaviour is geared towards your search for independence; your personality yearns to detach itself from its origins in order to plant its own roots, establish its own value systems, and asset its freedom of thought and action. You are opportunistic and unpredictable, traits which can be attributed to your ruling planetary body, Uranus.

Though blessed with immense reasoning capacity, Aquarius also possesses great intuition and unique prophetic insight, being concerned with the future, rather than what has been before or what is right now. This mind, in spite of its flashy insightfulness, can be surprisingly fixed and difficult to change. Aside from being stubborn, Aquarians are honest and broad-minded, helpful to others, friendly and sociable, and are eager to please. They can also be shy and unpredictable, but are generally thoughtful and outgoing, being very popular with their many friends and acquaintances. While Aquarians have plenty of sensitivity and passion, they believe emotion should be the servant, not the master, of the heart.

The energy of Aquarius holds the 'vision of the future', possessing a mind 'time telescope', and it is an effective agent of social change, stabilised and sophisticated thought processes, and the intellectual capacity to take Capricorn's ideas and break down the structures and boundaries that have been built around them.

You can be unpredictable at times, but you never act in an impetuous way. Everything you do is logical and thought out; rarely do you act without thinking or randomly. Aquarians know it's time to change before the others catch up, a quality which can be both your friend and your enemy; you are always on the mark and ahead of your time, but it can be also lonely out there in the futuristic time-space reality. Your ruling planet Uranus gives you thunderbolts of inspiration and compels you to act in ways that the world is never quite ready for. Nothing about your guardian planet is subtle or idle, and nor should it be, for your ruler needs you to wake the world up and make it smell the coffee, providing it with a sense of sudden liberation from the chains of restriction. You are the sign that is tasked with the jobs of breaking the bonds of debilitating conditions and freeing society from its out-dated thinking patterns. Essentially an iconoclast, you give the world an exhilarating vision of new, altered states - accompanied by the lessons that the view is much better from 'up there'.

Aquarius is the sign of the genius, which in one dictionary's definition, is simply 'an extraordinary intellectual and creative power'.

The top wave of the Aquarius symbol can be interpreted as standing for the higher mind, with the bottom wave standing for the rational mind. The Aquarian mind's function is to reform structure through vision, applying innovative ideas, and discovery. However, this mind does not dwell in the world of feelings and although well-versed about the human psyche and the human condition on an intellectual level, they rarely wander into the realm of emotions; this keeps the mind 'safe' because it is in its intellectualised position that you can reason with it, whereas feelings cannot be reasoned with, according to the Water Bearer at least.

This sign is one of the most enigmatic and idiosyncratic signs of the zodiac, and very few people will ever truly understand your motives, your outlook, your nature or your needs (with the exception of other Aquarians perhaps). Although you are cheerful and possess gifts of a high social order, you are also frequently unpredictable, and often surprise others by doing unusual or unexpected things. You have a detached, elusive quality which other people can never seem to pin down, being friendly and remote at the same time.

You seek to transform the culture and community through participation in clubs, organisations, groups and organisations, or through charitable or volunteer work. Your intellectual efforts are marshalled to improve society, and you are driven by a special brand of altruism that seeks not only tolerance, but full social integration, acceptance and inclusiveness.

You never feel the need to 'fit in' or agree with the crowd in order to be popular or liked, for you don't care very much what other people think about you, and this only adds to your power and mystique. Like Scorpio, another Fixed sign, you design your own yardsticks for success. Your cool aloofness, always present to some degree, is read as mysterious by more Earth-bound others.

Aquarius represents the vital spiritual power which renews and fertilises all things. However, close, fussy or overly intimate personal relationships may bother you because you are the sign of the global humanitarian, giving you the qualities of the Universal lover rather than a personal lover. In fact, you are more effective when functioning within a group, organisation or cause, than when operating within the confines of a personal relationship.

In more ways than one you are a law unto yourself and although you can be very friendly, you do not like to become too deeply involved with other people, even those close to you. You feel most at ease in friendships and relationships where you can keep your distance and independence from others, while still enjoying the pleasure of interactions and exchanges with those you love. For the most part a loner, you treasure your inner freedom far too much to be willing to surrender your whole self to anyone; a part of you has always to fly above and separate from others, in freer, clearer skies.

Aquarians are simple souls deep down, though most like to trick others into thinking they are complex, mysterious and confident, which is one of the many reasons why you are so misunderstood - which you really don't mind at all, as it allows only those who are perceptive enough to penetrate your veil to come close enough to see the real you.

Aquarians can easily become excitable, for they have a sensitive nervous system. There is an air of contemplative thoughtfulness about you, but this is often coupled with your tendency to talk and chatter and express yourself in every way possible, constantly thinking or speaking about what is going on in your busy mind. You can sometimes lose perspective of your Earthly limitations when making plans for the future, and can become impatient and despondent when your actions are hindered or restricted by surrounding circumstances. Being the natural revolutionary and progressive thinker, you are ever eager to overthrow the existing 'system' if it limits the implantation and actualisation of your many theories and visions in any way.

Aquarius is the bohemian of the zodiac, who will try anything at least once and sees nothing wrong with experimentation. The group spirit means a great deal to you, and the feeling of your personal merger with a higher ideal is akin to a religious experience for you. Multifaceted in your social life, you will often do unexpected things which are not sanctioned by the majority. Aquarians may even have a love/hate relationship with one of their associated areas: astrology. The reason for this is because this field, particularly Sun sign astrology, throws them together with other Aquarians, and this threatens their need to be different and individualistic, traits they protect with a deeply ingrained characteristic fixity.

The Aquarian is at its best when working with ideas. Your highest ambition is to make a better world, and this inspiration will keep you going through any obstacle or adversity. Not concerned with image, class or status, independence means more to the Aquarian soul than outward signs of success. You are the sign of the reformer, and this means that you are interested in new ideas, unorthodox trends and original ways of thinking. Independence, freedom in all its forms, individuality and even emotional isolation are necessary for Aquarians to shine their brightest. Sparkling ideas, when combined with emotion, can often become clouded or distorted, and Aquarius doesn't like its outlets or expression of ideas stifled in any way, hence you suppress or store your feelings somewhere else well out of the way. Indeed, Aquarians need to retire from the world at times and to become temporary loners in order to 'recharge' and renew themselves.

You can be temperamental when people or circumstances come into conflict with your many ideas. You can be tenacious when you decide on something, and the Fixed quality of Aquarius suggests that you will stubbornly refuse to budge if you are intent on doing something you truly believe to be right. The true Aquarian yearns to be the harbinger of enlightenment, but it is also important that in order to balance your desires and visions with reality, you need to understand that all men are *not* created equal, nor do they all share your conceptions and ideals. Your mission, instead, is to bring new ideas, inventions and social doctrines to the fore so that mankind may experiment with them and come to its own conclusions and solutions; you need only to deliver the 'facts', pouring forth the waters of knowledge from your urn, to start the wheels turning in the right direction.

Refusing to follow the crowd, you dislike interference by others, however helpfully intended, and will accept it only on your own terms; similarly, you may seek advice but will rarely heed it. Possessing strong and attractive personalities, Aquarius is nonetheless the most perplexing sign of the zodiac (a trait shared with Scorpio), and also the most individual and independent; your mind and body must both be as free as the wind.

You are adventurous without being foolhardy, and valiant and self-confident, surrounded by a certain aura of 'knowing', yet blessed with the absence of arrogance. You are unlikely to know defeat, certainly not permanently, and are rarely kept down for long by depression or setbacks.

Your personal style and appearance is usually distinctive and magnetic, attracting those who sense and appreciate your refreshingly quirky uniqueness. Aquarians are indeed unique, but curiously, never in the way everyone else is. Usually popular and well-liked, you are the archetypal good friend and all-rounder, enjoying people both individually and en masse, with a global perspective on humanity and the human condition, but also a gregarious nature towards those in closer circles, endearing you to most and on all levels.

You fall into two principal types: one shy, sensitive, gentle and patient; the other exuberant, lively and exhibitionist, sometimes hiding the substantial depths of your character under a veil of frivolity. Both types are strong-willed, forceful and have strong convictions, and although you seek truth above all things, you are usually honest enough to examine your opinions should you be mistaken in them. You have a breadth of vision, can see both sides of an argument and are unprejudiced and tolerant of others' points of view, even if you do not accept them yourself. In this way you are extremely objective, a quality endowed upon you by the Air element.

Humane, frank, serious minded, intelligent, concise, logical, clear, genial, refined, quick, active, persevering, sometimes ethereal, and ever idealistic, you express yourself with reason, moderation and often a dry brand of humour. Your nature can be difficult at times to pin down, for you are neither cynical nor naïve, neither enthusiastic nor complacent, neither assertive nor timid; and in more ways than one, contradictory.

The freedom-loving Water Bearer can be acutely funny, perverse, original, independent and conceited, but they can also be diplomatic, gentle, sympathetic and reserved. A certain cloud of isolation hangs over the Aquarian, and they are often misunderstood by others, and indeed mankind. That's because mankind hasn't yet caught up with the Aquarian way of thinking, and since your sign lives in the future, you can seem just plain odd and even a bit wacky to more Earth-bound, mundane souls. Your Aquarian mind senses this, and it just serves to deepen your sense of isolation, making you apt to wander among the lonely clouds, while the mere mortals around you wonder what you're doing out there - which is usually something along the lines of climbing rainbows, riding a shooting star, wishing upon a distant Sun, reminiscing about the future, re-shaping the past, dreaming up a utopia, swimming in optical illusory mirages, or visualising a society where there are not only round holes but an abundance of square ones too so that everyone may fit in.

However far ahead and out of reach you appear to be, it is always worthwhile for others to try to listen to what the Aquarian is effectively prophesising, for your flashes of insight into tomorrow and beyond have the potential to illuminate the world. Whether you are being social or want to be left strictly alone for periods of solitude and restoration, you'll retain your sharp perception, which is at once both deeper and quicker than everyone else's.

A curious mixture of coolness, charm, aloofness, practicality and eccentric instability, you seem to have an instinctive empathy and affinity with those on differing mind planes, such as the mentally unwell. It is because of your thinly veiled, highly acute nervous system that you have access to such levels of understanding.

You accept neither authority nor convention unless you can be satisfied that there are sound and convincing reasons for them. You see through pretentiousness and pomp and will energetically support causes, sometimes extreme, which oppose tradition, establishment and structure. You are too tolerant and intelligent to become an anarchic revolutionary crusader however, as ultimately you are an original and progressive thinker who seeks innovation and reform above all else, and like to go about it in an unassuming way. Not that you're modest, you are simply unmoved by glory, attention and limelight. Authority also leaves you unmoved and when faced with it, you will regard it with either indifference, deliberate rebellion or even a degree of friendliness or interest, but no amount of courtesy can prevent you from turning the spotlight of truth onto 'reality', for you possess profound integrity and a deep sense of right and wrong, justice and injustice.

You have a powerful desire for a lifestyle that is in some way unique, and are often so devoted to it, and so intent achieving and maintaining independence, that it can be difficult for you to commit to permanent relationships. Really 'knowing' an Aquarian is a matter for debate, for while people of this sign make very good, kind, helpful friends, it soon becomes clear that because they are so private no one really knows much about them. When questioned or cornered, you will usually evade the inquisitor's question or suspicion so successfully, effortlessly and charmingly that it slips by unnoticed - such is the elusive charm of Aquarius.

Although you appear absent-minded at times, your thinking is always razor sharp and crystal clear. You also possess an unequalled intuition which gives you a high degree of psychic precognition, and you seem to pick up on your own or others' desires without words, uncovering a need or quality buried so deep that you're even unaware of it yourself. This quality may be somewhat suppressed, however, so that you may get on with the more important business of helping humanity rather than meddling in the affairs of individuals, which holds no appeal to you. In Aquarius, where Universal rather than personal objectives are emphasised, the luminous, fiery temperament of the Sun is in its detriment, for the personal will and ego finds little fulfilment in a sign where all are deemed equal.

As well as a strong standing for equality, Aquarians have a great sense of fairness, courage in their ideas and convictions, and passion in their ideals, but by nature they are not very good at reading what's required on a more personal level and may acquire a reputation for being cold and insensitive; they are also prone to teeter on the edge of fanaticism. The Aquarian needs to learn, however, that it can create a prison for itself through its lack of emotional commitment, and deal with the apparent contradiction that freedom actually gains its wings through conscious commitment. To truly soar through the heavens, the Aquarian needs to reconcile this apparent paradox.

The fixed inflexibility of Aquarius is dedicated but uncompromising, for as much as you love change in society and the wider world, you stubbornly refuse to change your own ideas for anybody. Being an essential truth-seeker, you'll seldom tell an outward lie, but you can fool others in very subtle ways; in other words, you will be truthful to a fault, but Aquarian logic dictates that telling a lie is one thing, refraining from telling the whole story is quite another.

Aquarians get credit for being idealists, but you are too clever to be fooled by illusions, swayed by popular opinion, and you can certainly never be accused of blind faith and optimism. You will rarely fight a lost cause for too long, as, being the rational 'realist' that you are ensures your feet are always planted firmly in the ground. You do, however, believe sincerely that a little twisting and tweaking will improve anything, although you can easily be disappointed emotionally because your own high personal ideals cause you to demand more of others than is reasonable; and if disillusioned you may find it hard to forgive.

You are the subtle extremist and the paradoxes don't stop there: you can be a humanitarian or anarchist, protestor or peacemaker, society dropout or the society drop-in centre, genius or fanatic, reputable scientist or mad professor, rebel or social crusader, the liberated or the libertine - or all of the above at the same time! No wonder you make others dizzy and confused! The Aquarius is rarely confused however; rather it is those around it who are left spinning by its frenetic mental activity radiating outwards and electrifying those who are courageous enough to come in close enough to really feel it. But if those others do take the time to listen to you, they will actually catch a glimpse of the future, for it is here the true and pure Aquarius dwells.

Your humanitarian side is one of your most magnificent traits. You loathe bigotry and believe in accepting others for what and who they are, rather than for what religion they follow or the colour of their skin. You view life very clearly in this regard, and often from a perspective that's blindly obvious once you explain it properly to the mere mortals around you. In their human approach, Aquarians are the custodians of the future, the gatekeepers of destiny and the great thinkers of the zodiac, and everyone's life is richer for knowing you.

Aquarians usually possess an above average intelligence, enhanced by their inventive, progressive and futuristic thinking. The Air element expresses itself in Aquarius as aloof detachment and lack of deep personal involvement, which allows the Aquarian to indulge their eccentricities and spread their trademark friendliness even further. Being essentially detached and impersonal, expressions of deep feelings won't come easily to an Aquarian, and the line between love and friendship is all but invisible to the Water Bearer's soul. The Aquarian belongs to everyone, yet to no one; love can be wild and adventurous, but there will always be an elusive quality about it, and you will do everything you can to avoid great displays of intimacy.

From time to time, real brilliance can emerge from Aquarians, and anyone close to such individuals should be careful not to write them off as harmless eccentrics. Though rarely does an Aquarian see them self as an eccentric, just a little ahead of their time and not fully understood. Blessed with such an ingenious mind, you should develop your inborn originality, since you can be very creative. This, coupled with your need to have a distinctively individual lifestyle, unhindered by commitments and authority, are likely to provide your greatest motivations to succeed.

Aquarians can quite easily rise from obscurity to develop high-minded purposes and strong characters. Your self-reliance, gifted intellect, unique way of looking at things, understated confidence and your inner 'knowing' that you are right are assets which could be used to climb skyward. Indeed, these are the qualities that can lay the foundation of your success, and once your ambition is sparked, you are capable of scaling unprecedented heights.

You have a tendency to indolence however, and if you delay or treat life lazily, you will never achieve the great heights your mind is capable of achieving. Your unassuming nature and lack of boastfulness and ego are also assets which can be used to climb skyward. Ultimately, Aquarians are dedicated and humane champions to their causes, with strong ideals and convictions, and above all, forever seeking the truth - which always resides in tomorrow.

LESSONS TO BE LEARNED FOR GREATER POWER, ENLIGHTENMENT & LUCK

Aquarian problems and ultimate undoings arise through your contradictory nature, eccentricity, rebelliousness for its own sake, the desire for change to the detriment of all else, and your contradictory and paradoxical tendencies, which often leave others confused, bewildered and unable to rely upon you. Aquarius has two powerful rulers, Saturn being your traditional ruler and Uranus being your modern ruler; both planets exert their own unique influences, and most Aquarians will fall into one category or the other. Saturnian Water Bearers are inclined to be rigid, intense, severe, cool, controlling and may strive to attain their lofty ideals through anarchism. Uranian Water Bearers are unconventional, perverse, contrary and sometimes act up for the mere sake of being different - or difficult! Prone to mental disturbances, this type may also tend towards bouts of anarchy, annihilation, 'stirring the pot', conflicting with authority, shaking up establishments, and all-out rebellion. Indeed, that person who is willing to chain themselves to a tree to confront bulldozers is likely to be a Uranian type, or at the very least have a prominent Aquarius influence in their chart!

Your belief in individual freedom and your objectivity are the bases of both your strengths and weaknesses. Your deep love of humanity and freedom of expression can be empowered by your higher far-sighted mind. A strong social conscience impels you to give practical expression to your beliefs and to fight inequalities and hypocrisy in your daily life. However, your objectivity and visionary ideals can also lead to a self-indulgent sense of 'the world owes me'. Although generally altruistic and giving, you can tend towards selfishness and perverse lone wolf behaviour if you allow your garden of 'brotherhood' to grow too wild. Or this weakness may emerge in personal relationships where you can spout humanitarian theories but forget to show love, understanding and compassion to those closest to you. Fearing the loss of individuality can mean that you hold back from intimacy, yet your greatest fulfilment will occur when you put your heart before your intellect.

The challenge is to learn how to become more cooperative and involve others more in your idealistic goals; you tend to go it alone and usually do so with a stubborn, inflexible manner. If you learn how to reach inside and exude a bit more warmth and concern for others on a personal, individual level, and not just with regard for humanity or groups, you will evolve, grow, glow and simply flow - and maybe even be allowed to keep your rose-coloured glasses on as you go!

THE THREE DECANS OF AQUARIUS

Decans are thirty-six groups of stars that rise in a particular order on the horizon throughout each Earth rotation. These decans were developed in Egypt thousands of years ago. The rising of each decan marked the beginning of a new 'decanal hour' of the night for these ancient people, and eventually three decans were assigned to each zodiac sign. Each decan covers ten degrees of the zodiac wheel, and is ruled by different planetary rulers that rule over the other two signs of the same element (and a traditional ruler, when only seven of the planetary bodies were known). Decans continued to be used throughout the Ages, in astrology and in magic, but many modern astrologers, for whatever reasons, tend to disregard them. Following are brief descriptions for each decan of Aquarius. Which one do you belong to? Can you relate to the description and the energies of your decan's ruling planet?

FIRST DECAN AQUARIUS ★ January 20 - 30

Ruler ★ Venus (traditional *) / Uranus (modern)

Keyword ★ Original

First Decan Aquarius's Three Special Tarot Cards The Star, King of Swords & Five of Swords

Birthdays in this decan range from 21st to 30th January. This is the Aquarius decan, ruled by Venus * and Uranus. Aquarians born during this decan possess an original, inventive mind which comes up with innovative ideas and engages in progressive thinking. Your concepts, views and beliefs are often seen as unusual, futuristic or avant-garde. Venus as the traditional ruler for this decan, makes you both lucid and serious, understanding and lenient. In relationships, your behaviour is always original, and your motivations are vital and occasionally changeable. You thrive when around many other people and shine your brightest when you are at parties and social gatherings. You love meeting new people, enjoying new experiences, and are attractive and fascinating to others, who you easily entrance and beguile with your uniqueness, wit and charm. You dislike being constrained by conventions and personal relationships, and need regular time by yourself in your own inner world. You may come across as weird or eccentric to others, and always live truthfully and unwaveringly by your own unique code.

SECOND DECAN AQUARIUS ★ January 31 - February 9

Ruler ★ Mercury (traditional *) / Mercury (modern)

Keyword ★ Inspirational

Second Decan Aquarius's Three Special Tarot Cards The Star, King of Swords & Six of Swords

Birthdays in this decan range from 31st January to 9th February. This is the Gemini decan, ruled by Mercury *. Aquarians born during this decan have good reasoning ability, a ready wit, and an ability to reach out to people with a mental and intellectual approach. The Dark Moon, being an alternative ruler of this decan, exalts your need for independence, moral and emotional freedom, and imagination. You often experience vivid inspirations, and when your imagination is unleashed, you can go from dream to reality without transition. You are likely to be changeable, versatile and enjoy variety and change. This influence also makes you imaginative, honest, open and smart, and an analytical thinker who makes decisions based on your head rather than your heart. Naturally academic and scholarly, you love study, both formal and informal (incidental) and you tend to live your life at a fast pace, preferring quick results to whatever you apply your mind to. Second decan Aquarians are characterised by openness, sociability and imagination, making you a gifted communicator and excellent at pursuits such as creative writing. You can use the power of words to your advantage, getting your message across eloquently and convincingly. Intelligent, clear-thinking and quick-witted, what others see is what they get with you, as you have no hidden agenda; Aquarian frankness and 'truth' is at its purest under the influence of clever Mercury, and you are always one step ahead of others in your thinking.

THIRD DECAN AQUARIUS ★ February 10 - 19

Ruler ★ Moon (traditional *) / Venus (modern)

Keyword ★ Idealistic

Third Decan Aquarius's Three Special Tarot Cards The Star, Knight of Cups & Seven of Swords

Birthdays in this decan range from 10th February to 19th February. This is the Libra decan, ruled by the Moon * and Venus. Aquarians born during this decan are characterised by impulsivity, charm and romanticism. With a constant need for social stimulation and excitement, you love to explore many fascinating ideas and interests. You are naturally swept away towards utopian, avant-garde and occasionally brilliant ideas. A natural romantic, love plays a big part in your life, and you are charming and magnetising, attracting many admirers to you, but your need for change and your natural restlessness can prove a challenge to achieving sustained long-term relationships. Bright, breezy and charismatic, you enjoy attention from others and sharing your thoughts, affection and concepts. Being so mysterious and intriguing, many will try and figure you out, but very few will succeed, for your true nature is often hidden. You are the most sensitive and emotional of the Aquarian decans, and although easily bored, you are unerringly generous to those you love, and will always give your time, love and energy to them unconditionally.

* The decan's traditional ruler based on the Chaldean order of the planets

YOUR ELEMENT ★ AIR

According to the *Oxford English Dictionary*, the word *element* has a mysterious origin, and was first found in Greek texts meaning 'complex whole' or 'a single unit made up of many parts'. From the ancient up to medieval times, there were only four elements - Earth, Air, Fire and Water - and the occult-oriented also believed in a fifth: Spirit, or Ether. (Cornelius Agrippa called Spirit the 'quintessence'.)

Alchemy is a tradition of visions and dreams, and images can combine on different levels of reality. Alchemists have long used images in their illustrations to express the enigma and mystery of their art, and to include all dimensions of our experience. The traditional worlds of Earth, Water, Fire and Air symbolise these dimensions very well. Broadly speaking, and in human terms, Earth corresponds to the level of the body and the senses, Water to the flow of thoughts and feelings, Fire to inspiration and energy, and Air to the world of the higher mind. Each of these worlds has its own realm of imagery. Aquarius belongs to the realm of the Air element.

★ The Intellectual Group ★

The path to BROTHERHOOD

Focused on Mental & Social Interactions

Alchemical Associations ★ The Intellect, Gold and the Colour Yellow

Key Attributes ★ Communication, Intelligence, Reason, Perspective, Renewal, Thought, Logic

Symbolism ★ Clear Thought, Communication, Study, Connection to the Universals

Governed by ★ The Mind and the Psyche

Air Characteristics ★ Intelligent, Wise, Thoughtful, Analytical, Detached, Objective

★ THE MAGIC OF AIR ★

Many Eastern philosophies believe that the vital force that energises both humans and the cosmos is carried in the Air, entering our bodies when we breathe. This fundamental energy is called *prana* in India, *chi* in China and *ki* in Japan. Spiritual prayers from Buddhist prayer flags are believed to be carried in the wind.

Air is invisible and intangible, but it drives life and is necessary to animate all living things. Represented by sky, wind, flight and breath, Air can be a cool breeze, fanning the flames of desire, or a strong wind, creating a hurricane. Taking deep breaths can calm and soothe the spirits. Air represents your intellect - the ambitions that are driven by a cool detachment from your emotions. Air seeks out what you need more than what you want and fans you gently along, rather than sweeps you off your feet with the dreams, force or illusions of Water or Fire; Air rationalises your desires. It also refreshes and purifies you, blowing away your problems and carrying you towards new solutions - by being literally a 'breath of fresh air' in your experiences.

★ KEYWORDS ★

Broad-minded, fair, objective, refined, ideas-oriented, communicative, observant, versatile, rational, theoretical, social, learning-oriented, impersonal, logical, innovative, connective, detached, active-minded, clever, curious, impartial, cooperative, abstract, integrating, networking, analytical, relationship-oriented, intellectual

Air is the mental principle. The most intellectual and innovative of the four elements, it is unconcerned with the material side of life, but rather it seeks to share with and communicate ideas to others. It is a connective energy, driven to share thought and mental rapport. Air is associated with the thinking function and its motivating force is mind-thought stimulation. Characterised by intellect and aspiration over passion, Airy types are ideas people, using rational and logical thought processes, seeking mental understanding and experiencing life through the mind. They are also objective and 'head-orientated', sometimes to the detriment of their emotions and intuition.

The three Air signs are Gemini the Twins, Libra the Scales and Aquarius the Water Bearer. In the horoscope wheel, Gemini represents personal development, Libra represents interpersonal development, and Aquarius represents transpersonal development. The Air signs, living in world of communication and the intellect, express themselves in these differing ways: Gemini, through its quickness to see both sides of any issue and to create original thoughts from what has been learned; Libra, through its ability to balance many different viewpoints and find a harmonious consensus and keep the status quo; and Aquarius, through its foresight and vision to understand the Universal principles that can be used for the betterment of mankind. The Air signs are masculine in polarity, extroverted in expression, and are aligned with the realms of relationships and connections of all kinds.

Air is perhaps the most misunderstood of the elements, because of its intangible nature and lack of visible manifestation. However, without Air there can be no Fire; Water devoid of oxygen is merely hydrogen gas; and in the absence of Air there is simply no conscious, breathing life. Air represents the insubstantial state of mind of cognisance. As a progressive chain of development, Elemental Air is the final stage of spiritual evolution. Fire is the first creative spark, which coalesces into the nurturing Waters of life and growth, Earth the solid, corporeal plane of existence, but as all life is cyclical and these material states eventually wane and waste away, Elemental Air remains as the soul-like auric energy or discarnate spirit. Additionally, Air is usually invisible and one only notices its effects when it is directed through another element. Indeed, Air's magical powers can be activated through Fire (smoke), Earth (moving through mobiles and wind chimes for example), and Water (inhalation, steam and vaporisation).

Air gives us life, thanks to that which we breathe in. It is both life- and death-inducing, very real and yet ambiguous. In astrology, the exact moment the newborn inhales its first breath is when we choose to establish the birth chart. But this rhythm of life is also a rhythm of death. In fact, the breath which enables a child to live independently and freed from its cord, depends on a continuous movement. At the other end of life, withholding your breath signifies drawing your last and expiring, or dying. Ultimately, breathing is a spontaneous, instinctive, vital action which allows us to exist.

The soul and breath have always been closely linked. But breath is not the soul; it is its vehicle. Both are unseen and impalpable. Breath is also the vehicle for thought, sound, spirit, speech and language. Air is the same for everyone, yet our breath is unique to us alone. Perhaps that is why those born of the Air element often have a delicate albeit superficial sensitivity to the Air around them, its nuances and temperature, its feel and its nature, its fragrance and its moisture.

Air is also associated with inspiration, ideas and exchange, representing the Divine energies and messages from the gods. Inspired by birds, shamans use spirit flight in their healing ceremonies and rituals. Air can open your mind to new possibilities and allow your imagination to take flight. All cultures have legends of wise 'messengers' descending from the air, such as angels, birds, winged dragons and science fiction aliens, all of whom, it is supposed, have access to higher sources of information than Earth-dwellers. Witches are often depicted flying through the Air on their broomsticks, a symbol of their wisdom and magic. And the sky gods of ancient times were all guardians of arcane studies and were thought to pass on these gifts to the humans who believed in as well as called upon them.

When we work with Air, we think of the Divine breath of spirit, the ability to move through space and time, and the wisdom derived from experience and study. Like the other elements, Air has three manifestations - mental, astral and physical - when used in magic and ritual. We can visualise (mental), request the use of the energy (astral), or physically create the Elemental associations in our experience. Where Earth elemental magic lends itself to manifesting things in a physical form, finding treasure, creating abundance and harnessing the strength within, Air is more of a studious, mental variety: writing and telling stories, sending messages, taking (mental) notes, composing music, studying anything, and clarity of thought. Hermes, the Greek messenger god, and his Roman counterpart Mercury are both associated with the Air element.

The Air element is connected to understanding, intellectual concepts, innovations, insight, mental rapport, technology, synthesising information, ideas, communication, and knowledge. As air has no boundaries, it can be difficult for this element to accept boundaries established by others. It is objective, gives a sense of separation through interdependence, is sophisticated and is linked to the past, present *and* future. It seeks intellectual rapport and stimulation above all else, and has a conscious sense of *knowing*.

This element is detached, impersonal, separate, represents breath and life, is an ideas perfectionist, is judging, assessing, collating, paradoxical, space-seeking, freedom-seeking, flighty, has an approach/avoidance element, develops ways to communicate, is an observer/spectator, gossiper, is an excellent witness to the human experience, is an equality-idealist, is dual-natured in many ways, has difficulty with intimacy, is dissociative in the face of challenge, is aware and conscious, has an urge to relate and 'share', is socially inclined and witty, has perspective, keeps its distance, is changeable, fair, learned, inspiring and opinionated, and has an attitude of "knowledge is power."

Airy temperaments excel at clear, objective reasoning and have a capacity for lively, intelligent communication and the exchange of ideas. These types are gregarious, civilised, curious, cooperative, casual, fun-loving and sociable.

However, they can be overly intellectual, objective and rational, uncomfortable with feelings, and too often trust their heads before their hearts. Other weaknesses that may trip them up occasionally are that they have a tendency to be scattered, unfocused, unrealistic, detached, distant, impersonal, nervous, unstable, inconsistent, spacey, erratic, whimsical, fickle, impractical, superficial, opinionated, dogmatic, impulsive, skittish, 'mercurial', disembodied, a chatterbox, have an overactive mind and can't be tied down.

As the element suggests, Airy spirits are constantly on the move, shifting, changing and evolving. Air signs are generally unnerved by states of flux, as movement is a chance for growth and exploration to these inquisitive souls. Independent, open-minded and spontaneous, Air signs loathe restrictions and anything which curtails their freedom, especially of thought. They love to broaden their horizons through circulating amongst people, places and experiences, as understanding others and their surroundings is paramount to making sense of their existence.

Air signs rely heavily on reason, logic and objectivity. This enables the cerebral Air signs to make fair and objective assessments, but this intellectualisation of thought and feeling can also make them come across as detached and unemotional. As they have a strong need for novel and perpetual stimulation, Air signs tend to be restless and can suffer from nerve-related upsets. But blessed with outgoing and naturally expressive personalities, they are highly sociable as well as good communicators. Air signs enjoy the company of others and love engaging in hearty, interesting conversations through which they can gain knowledge and swap ideas. Impartial by nature, they often make great mediators in relationships or families and having an upbeat, generally uncomplicated nature means Air signs also have a natural talent for diffusing tense situations and lifting the spirits of others.

Positive Air Qualities ★ Focused on ideas and their expression, objective, tolerant, inspiring, articulate, socially adept, intelligent, cooperative, stimulating, charming, rational, relational, mentally clear, succinct, detached, perceptive, sharp, clever, gregarious, and capable of forethought, understanding and the grasping of abstract concepts.

Negative Air Qualities ★ Impractical, unemotional, lacking in sympathy, glib, non-committal, facile, hyperactive, nervous, dissociated from the body and the physical world, manipulative, flighty.

THE ARCHANGEL OF AIR ★ RAPHAEL

An archangel is an angel of greater than ordinary rank. They possess a stronger, more powerful essence than the guardian angels, through overseeing and guiding the other angels who are said to be with us here on Earth. The word 'angel' derives from the Greek word *angelos* meaning 'messenger'. To humans, angels are often seen as bringers as all sorts of messages. Angels in all their forms are believed to bring the message of 'spirit' into matter, carrying the blueprints of creation and the Source from the Divine into the manifest world. Angels are not and never have been human; they, like fairies and nature spirits, are part of a different evolutionary pattern – but they do appear to us in human form (usually with wings) because that is what we understand. An angel can be in many different places at once, and with the same intensity and concentration, and wish for us to be aware of them and benefit from them.

There are said to be three categories of angels in the cosmos, each with three subdivisions *. 'Angel' is the generic term and also relates specifically to those closest to the physical. Similarly, archangel may be taken to mean any of the higher orders, and indeed signifies the order just above ordinary 'angel'. Found in a number of religious traditions, the word 'archangel' itself is usually associated with the Abrahamic religions. The word archangel is of Greek origin, and means literally 'chief angel'. All archangels end with the 'el' suffix, 'el' meaning 'in God' and the first part of the name meaning what each individual Angel specialises in. The archangel who rules your sign will be the one with whom you most resonate. The astrological sign is an energy signature, a matrix of a specific stellar pattern that will subtly affect and influence you. Although there are many associations for the great archangels of the Universe, we must keep in mind there is great overlapping in their duties and guidance. For example, we may say that one is for healing and another for protection, but they can all perform the functions of the others, and each has only areas of greater focus and responsibilities. Four of the multitude of archangelic beings work intimately with the Earth. These are Raphael (Air), Michael (Fire), Gabriel (Water) and Uriel (Earth). Associated with each of these archangels are one of the four elements, specific colours, one of the four directions or quarters of the Earth, three signs of the zodiac, and a variety of other energies and powers. Understanding these associations and considering them in relation to our own paths, can help us determine with which of them we are more likely to resonate. Your sign, being of the Air element, vibrates to the essence of Raphael.

* The first sphere, the *Heavenly Counsellors*, comprises Seraphim, Cherubim and Thrones. The second sphere, the *Heavenly Governors*, comprises Dominions, Virtues and Powers. The third sphere, the *Heavenly Messengers*, comprises Principalities, Archangels and Angels. Of course, all such classifications are a human construct, a way of placing order upon the unknowable and allowing us to perceive something about which we have no words to express. However, as long as we think of angelic hierarchies as a way of working with celestials, of remembering important attributes, and we are able to imagine and experience these beings, this order of angels will prove useful to those wishing to draw upon their messages and assistance.

★ ARCHANGEL RAPHAEL'S ASSOCIATIONS ★

Element of Air
The eastern quarter of the Earth
The spring season
The colour blue (or blue and gold)
The astrological signs of Gemini, Libra and Aquarius

Raphael, meaning "Healing power of God" or "The Divine has healed," is the archangel of healing and safe travels. This being works to stimulate energies for overall life and success. Raphael awakens a sense of beauty, wonder and creativity which stimulates higher mental faculties. He is the supreme healer in the angelic realm, whose chief role is to support, heal and guide in all matters of health, working to heal people's minds, bodies and spirits so they can enjoy overall peace and wellbeing. Raphael is the Keeper of the Holy Grail.

AQUARIUS'S ZODIAC ARCHANGEL ★ URIEL

Additionally, each sign is associated with a particular archangel. Such knowledge can help you to build up a relationship with these beings, based upon your strengths and needs. However, no link is rigid, and as you work with angels you will come to develop your own affinities. When invoking a specific archangel, a useful ritual to draw them closer is to light a candle in that angel's colour, burn some oil or incense of its scent, and hold the appropriate crystal while focusing on what you are needing guidance on.

YOUR ARCHANGEL ★ Uriel means 'fire of God' and he is linked with lightning, thunder and sudden happenings. He may be depicted carrying a scroll that contains revelations about your true path in life. Uriel is dynamic, and his gifts are stamina, action, dynamism and dispelling fears. Stimulating physical desires, call on Uriel if you are feeling desperate, depleted or rejected and he will help to restore your vitality and get you back on your feet.

SCENT/OIL ★ Clove

CANDLE COLOUR ★ Ruby red

CRYSTAL ★ Carnelian or red jasper

THE DEVIC REALMS & AIR ★ EAST: REALM OF THE SYLPHS

"Through magick we do conjure the Elements, evoking unto us the special properties of the Life-force for our learning and our coming-into-light. And yet are there secret paths of knowledge that have fallen from the minds of men ... For the way of Magick is a path to sacred knowledge, of reverence and humility - and the world is a wondrous place. Yet how many amongst us have fathomed these depths?"
***Merlin's Book of Magick and Enchantment*, Nevill Drury**

Deva is a Sanskrit word that means 'shining one'. Devas are the life force within nature, and there are four devic realms - Fire, Earth, Air and Water - which contain ethereal elemental spirits or sprites. Elementals are the building blocks of nature, and close to being true energy and consciousness. The four elements correspond to four different states of matter: energy/transmutation (Fire), gas (Air), liquid (Water) and solid (Earth), which are linked to the four human states of consciousness: inspiration, thought, feeling and practicality. There are four spirits, or elementals, which reside in the devic realms, associated with each element. People have been painting pictures, telling stories and writing about these devic realms for hundreds of years, albeit sometimes through disguised mediums such as fairy tales or children's fantasy stories like Tolkien's *Lord of* *the Rings*. The power of the natural world is easily observed and since ancient times primal forces have been ascribed to various spirit beings. Belief in nature spirits is of such ancient origin and is Universal; cultures everywhere have names or words to describe them. In the sixteenth century, a famous Swiss physician, alchemist and mystic called Paracelsus * defined these beings as 'Elementals', classifying them according to the element of nature they inhabit. There are four main levels of elemental beings: Gnomes (Earth), Undines (Water), Sylphs (Air), and Salamanders (Fire). The fifth element of Ether is the element from which came forth the other four, and Ether, or Spirit, has never been defined in any particular category, and encompasses the aspects and beings of all the other elements.

Elementals are usually benevolent guardian beings or spirits that look after nature's secrets and treasures in whatever part of the natural realm they occupy. They can only be seen or 'felt' by those possessing heightened psychic abilities, yet they can be summoned by those practising alchemy, spells and magic in order to harness the forces of nature for their own particular intentions. In our modern lives, it may seem as though this magic doesn't exist, but the truth is that most of us are simply less in touch with it than ever before. The consequence of this is that we are destroying vast areas of land, polluting waters, creating toxic landscapes, and disrespecting the laws of nature, which often whisper their messages softly. It is therefore important for us to look at the beauty that surrounds us with true appreciation and genuine regard, and to open ourselves up to the magic resides within it. The four devic realms can teach us much about nature; they act as custodians for the four elements, and learning to work with them is a way of attuning to all the energies and beings of nature. Elementals are four-dimensional, and have nothing to obstruct their movements. Therefore, they move as easily through matter as we do through air and space. They do require some contact with humans for their own evolution. Helping to direct them is an overseer, traditionally called the King of that element, and an archangel. Each of these elements is affiliated with one of the four directions and each elemental spirit embodies its own special energy. If you wish to re-connect and re-harmonise yourself by working with nature and its messages and lessons, you could begin by learning a little about your element's realm: Your element is Air, which is connected with the East direction and the realm of the Sylphs.

* Paracelsus is considered the most original medical thinker of the sixteenth century. His belief in supernatural beings, intuition and the invisible causes of illness helped him discover hydrogen and nitrogen. Paracelsus believed that "Elementals are unlike pure spirits for they are mortal, but they are not like man for they have no soul."

★ SYLPHS ★

Sylph is from the Greek *silphe*, and the word means 'butterfly'; these spirits control all winds. Sylphs are fairy-like spirits that inhabit the air, winds and atmosphere as well as high mountain tops (not all sylphs are restricted to living in the air, however). They are probably more closely in line with our concept of fairies and angels than the other elemental beings; and indeed, they work alongside the angels. Always active and extremely quick of movement and sound, Air Elementals are also known to be highly intelligent as they can gather vast amounts of information in a short period of time. They are aloof and detached and usually very subtle in their persuasiveness. People with strong sylph influence or activity often find that sexuality is not high on their list of priorities, and may not understand how it can be so with others. But the sylphs stimulate the expression of the creative sexual drive into other avenues of one's life, such as work or hobbies.

The sylphs are guardians of spring, the direction of the east and the wind. Therefore, they are chiefly concerned with communication, the mind, the intellect and the kingdom of the feathered and winged creatures. As the east is the doorway to new beginnings and the direction through which the sacred circle is always entered, air has a uniquely ethereal, otherworldly, wispy quality to it. It makes its presence felt through its four winds: the north brings cold and withering; the east brings new life and freshness; the south brings vitality and warmth; and the west brings fertility and gentle abundance. Air, and its various components, is our vital life force, enabling us to exist. It also supports that which flies - from birds to human-made technology. It allows fire to burn and for communication with others and with the ether to flow with ease, and stimulates our intellect so we can exercise good reason, judgment and rational thought to enhance our lives. Air makes its home in the heavens and yet it flows freely as a gift for all to share. It moves among us like an unseen visitor, giving us life and strength, and carrying our wishes into the breeze for them to return in the form of free-flowing bounty in our physical world. Air inhabits our hearts, bring joy and wisdom and knowing, and sylphs guard these mind treasures as they are pure spirits of truth and beauty whose ways are not sullied by Earthly restrictions. The King of Air is Lugh or Paralda, its archangel is Raphael, its magickal tool is the athame (which calls down the spirits into form), and its sacred ceremonial stones are Lapis Lazuli, Sapphire, Blue Topaz and Azurite. Perhaps Merlin sums up the sylph realm best: "For these beings are like unto jewels of light, their wings glistening as crystal butterflies in the first Dawn. We may see them in a dance of light upon a leaf or petal, perchance amidst the forest dells or in the hidden glades where few have ventured."

INVOKING THE AIR DEVAS

Sylphs are best contacted in high, open spaces where the wind blows freely. They can be found in wind, clouds, rain, storms, and snowflakes. If you are in need of clearer thought and memory, greater freedom or better communication skills, ask the air devas for their help. They can help guide you if you have an important exam or journey to undertake, if you have to give a speech, or if you are doing anything that requires clear, swift thought and self-expression. To make contact with a sylph, make or acquire a dream catcher. A Native American craft, usually hoop-shaped with dangling beads and feathers, these are designed to 'catch' bad dreams and protect you while you sleep. Dream catchers can be adapted to attract sylphs however, although they can never really be caught, since they embody the essence of liberty and unencumbered flight. Perhaps you could get a new dream catcher for this very purpose, and imbue it with your positive intentions through a special affirmation. When you become aware of your sylph stirring your dream catcher, ask for the specific help you are requiring, thank the sylph for his or her help, then set them free back into their realm of flight and freedom, knowing that their help has been given and their work done. Sylphs also respond well to the burning of incense and music.

THE EAST DIRECTION'S CORRESPONDENCES

If you wish to work more with your particular element and direction, the following may help propel your wishes and magical journey:

Time of Day ★ Dawn
Polarity ★ Male, positive
Exhortation ★ To *will*
Musical Instruments ★ Wind instruments, harp
Colours ★ Gold, white
Season ★ Spring
Magical Instrument ★ Wand
Altar Symbol ★ Incense
Communion Symbol ★ Scent

Archangel ★ Raphael
Human Senses ★ Hearing, smell
Art Forms ★ Poetry Painting
Animals ★ Birds, bats
Mythical Beast ★ Winged horse
Magical Arts ★ Divinations
Guide Forms ★ Sky/weather gods
Meditation ★ Sky, clouds
Images & Themes ★ Mountain tops, flying, sunrise, wisdom and knowledge

HOW YOU CAN GET IN TOUCH WITH YOUR AIR ENERGY

"When we are present with and summon the magic of Air, we gain wings"

★ Use Air energy when making wishes around the following: Travel, exam success and study, job interviews, meditation, relaxation, more effective communication with others, improved expression and articulation of needs, mental stability, increasing knowledge-base, nervous stress relief

★ In magical practices, Air can be represented by smoke, which can be created by burning a joss stick or incense. The following tools and methods can also be used to carry your dreams to the skies and ether: Feathers, hanging mobiles in the breeze with your wishes attached, paper darts, autumn leaves, and airborne seeds

★ The best days on which to employ Air magic are Wednesdays, ruled by the planet of communication Mercury, or Thursdays, ruled by Thor, the Norse god of thunder. If possible, choosing a windy day with gales or thunderstorms will make your work more powerful. Air spells are also most effective when performed beneath an open sky; a high mountain would be an ideal location. Writing a wish on a kite or a balloon and guiding it through the air, as high as possible, by a piece of string can harness the magic of the Air spirits, who will help you clarify and manifest your desires, through quite literally releasing your wish into the wind

★ Spend time in open, fresh, clean air regularly

★ Spend time in wide open spaces and engage in outdoor activities that make use of the air around you, such as flying a kite or ballooning

★ Learn Prana-, Chi- or Ki-related disciplines, martial arts, meditation and yoga that focus on breathing, focus, mental-detachment and concentration

★ Read as much as you can; be an eternal student

★ Blue-coloured crystals will activate your connection with the element of Air and enhance your dreams, soothe your fears, calm your nervous system, help you communicate, bring about inner peace, and assist in self-transformation

★ Develop your networking skills

★ Throw intellectual dinner parties

★ Join a discussion group or an online Internet chat room

★ Practice deep breathing

★ Learn about meteorology, cloud formations, the atmosphere and the weather

★ Use a negative ion machine, humidifier or air purifier in your home

★ Don't smoke, or if you do, quit (being associated with the lungs, Geminis should particularly take note of this)

★ Sleep on an air mattress

★ Meditate on the Swords suit in the Tarot (the Swords suit represents the Air element)

★ Take a course - in anything and everything!

★ Know a little bit about everything; trivia is more powerful than its given credit for!

★ Write; keep a journal

★ Visit the library on a regular basis; join a book discussion group

★ Look after your lungs, other components of your respiratory system, and your nervous system

★ Take a course, learn a language, or otherwise make a commitment to a learning activity which requires discipline, focus and mental energy

★ Take a course on improving your relationships

★ Hire a jumping castle and invite your friends over!

★ Jump on a trampoline

★ Practice public speaking often, even solo in front of a mirror

★ Forget your mind chatter and allow your heart to lead occasionally; it always knows where to go

★ When working with the Air element in magical practice, stand at the East quarter of your magical space, as the East is its domain, and invite its living essence into your 'circle'

★ Air spirits are also known as air devas, zephyrs, builders or sylphs, and can be called upon to calm our nerves, cleanse our thoughts, clear anxiety and fear, and to help us focus with greater mental clarity, so Air signs would be wise to adopt one (or all) as their very own spirit guide!

YOUR MODE ★ FIXED

Each sign belongs to one of the three quadruplicities, Cardinal, Fixed and Mutable. If we closely examine the Earth's yearly cycle, we can form a very accurate picture of the nature of these quadruplicities, for they correspond directly with the manifestation of the seasons. Each season has three months: the first month brings the new phase of the cycle, the second month brings a concentration of the season's energy to its fullest expression, and the third month represents the transition from the current season to the next one. The astrological quadruplicities represent the three basic qualities in all life: creation (Cardinal), perseverance (Fixed) and destruction (Mutable). Every thing that is born, from a period of time to a human being, experiences a life and then dies. In this context, death can be taken to mean that the form of the energy changes; but the energy itself can never be annihilated, for form is mortal, whereas essence is immortal.

The Fixed mode covers the signs Taurus, Leo, Scorpio and Aquarius, and is the most determined and unshakable of the three qualities. The positive side of the Fixed signs is stability. You are the builders, whether of Earthly creations (Taurus), artistic endeavours (Leo), occult powers (Scorpio), or world-changing visions and ideas (Aquarius).

The Fixed mode signifies the manifestation of purpose and its subjects are concerned with ownership, concentration, stability, fixation, and working with a cool head and calm demeanour under pressure. The Fixed quality is associated with stabilisation, depth, preservation, persistence, loyalty and strength of will. You operate with purpose, dedication, self-reliance and determination, happy to forge ahead, through calmly working away, until you have achieved your ultimate goals. Fixed signs are a fearsome, formidable and quietly forceful group, able to follow their will and demonstrate fixity, often to the point of being stubborn, win-at-all-costs and wilful. Rarely are you distracted in your quests, for you have the ability to stay on firm course and track until a project's end. You are enduring, deliberate, steady and stable, but may be rigid and single-minded. You have a strong sense of routine, ritual and control. You work hard to consolidate and preserve the things that matter to you, but you can also be inflexible and resistant to change. You stick with situations even when they are outworn, uphold the status quo, and are loyal and dependable, but hate to give in and may lack spontaneity. Your energy and nature is powerful, robust, concrete, limited, set in its ways, purposeful, conscientious, slow, consistent, enduring, stubborn, innately cautious, rigid, unimpulsive, opinionated, unchanging, and you are generally strong in opinions, habits, likes and dislikes. Not easily distracted, you always keep your eyes on the prize, but you have a tendency to brood or to become stuck in a rut. You also project an image of strength as an effective shield against your considerable vulnerability. The Fixed mode indicates the midpoints of the seasons, which are very strong ritualistic times and 'fixed points', signifying points of power in the zodiac. Because Fixed signs fall in the middle of the season, this term signifies that the season is firmly established - fixed - by the time the Sun enters these signs.

Aquarius is the most rebellious and unpredictable of the Fixed signs, and will desperately try to do things its own way and on its own terms, with a 'lone-wolf' style fixity of purpose, even if it's suggested there is a better way - and *especially* if it's suggested there is a better way. This perseverance and determined attitude, while noble and courageous, can be isolating to the individual.

YOUR RULING PLANET ★ URANUS

The Great Awakener & Divine Rebel

Planetary Meditation
I am my Earth (my body),
and my Sky (my transcendence)
I am my Sun (my spirit),
and my Moon (my soul)
I am my Venus (my pleasure),
and my Jupiter (my faith)
I am my Mars (my courage),
and my Saturn (my lessons)
I am my Mercury (my thoughts),
and my Uranus (my truth)
I am my Neptune (my dreams),
and my Pluto (my transformation)

Each planet has its own distinctive and original meaning which, according to its position in the zodiac, combines with the qualities that are inherent in each of the twelve astrological signs. If a planet is your sign's ruler, however, it exerts a significant influence upon your life, regardless of its birth chart or zodiacal position.

Numbers ★ 4 and 22

Basic Energy & Magic ★ Invention, Innovation, Change

Colours ★ Light Blues, Electric & Glaring Hues, Stripes

Metal ★ Uranium

Gems/Minerals ★ Amber, Jacinth, Jargoon, Chalcedony, Aquamarine, Azurite, Sapphire, Lapis Lazuli

Zodiacal Influences ★ Rules Aquarius; Exalted in Scorpio; Detriment Leo; Fall Taurus

Transcendental ★ Associated with Change, Disruption and Shock ★ 84 Year Cycle

★ KEY WORDS ★
Intuition, electrifying force, innovation, disruption, higher or psychic functions, individuality, cosmic consciousness, inventions, shock, sudden or unexpected change, originality, electricity, revolution!

★ KEY CONCEPTS ★
★ The intuitive faculties, the Sixth Sense ★
★ The bohemian, the beatnik, the hippie, the nonconformist ★
★ The inventor, the 'mad scientist', the revolutionary, the anarchist ★
★ Destroyer of old ideologies, ways of life, concepts and structures ★
★ The global crusader, the social reformer ★
★ The embracer of Brotherhood, the humanitarian ★
★ The force for the awakening of the higher consciousness: individually, collectively and Universally ★

★ He who marches to the beat of his own drum ★

Uranus was discovered during the American and French revolutions, and the Industrial Revolution, in 1781, correlating it with the social themes of the time: freedom, independence, technological advancement, cultural innovation, revolution and rebellion. It is therefore fitting that Uranus, which sits beyond Saturn, should represent a break from tradition and barriers, and a certain emancipation from the structures and order that Saturn imposes. Discovered by musician and astronomer William Herschel, Uranus was at first believed to be a comet until further investigation confirmed its planetary nature. Its discovery was a startling revelation for the fields of astronomy and astrology, as the two disciplines believed the Solar system extended only to the limit of Saturn's orbit.

The glyph (or symbol) for Uranus is a cross with a circle suspended from the lower arm and a semi-circle attached to each of the side arms of the cross, reminiscent of a television aerial, symbolising Uranus's resonance with electricity and innovative communication technologies such as computers.

Uranus offers a welcome change from its neighbouring planet Saturn, giving us a chance to seize our freedom, break free, be progressive and enhance our creativity. Uranus is an astronomical maverick, alone in rotating horizontally, and on a personal level, its electrically charged energy is reckoned to denote individualists, reformers, outsiders and intellectual brilliance; people who break the norms of a cultural or political mould. People born under the sign of Aquarius are particularly sensitive to its influence, and being born with an (often) emphasised Uranus factor makes them susceptible to being extremely stimulated most of the time, living in a constant state of wired or otherworldly energy.

Its glyph, derived from H for Herschel, the surname of its discoverer, looks uncannily like an early television aerial, hence its link with televisions and other signal-receiving or electronic gadgetry. Uranus has also been handed the rulership of astrology itself, which may be due to the similarity of Uranus' name with that of Urania, the Greek muse of astronomy and astrology. Indeed, a powerfully aspected or placed Uranus in one's horoscope, is flourished as a powerful totem by astrologers.

Uranus is an erratic planet, orbiting on its axis at a 90-degree angle, different from the way everything else in the Solar system behaves, giving a good allusion to the nature of the Uranian mind: a different way of 'spinning' to almost everything and everyone around it. The Aquarian mind seems to have adopted this quirk from its ruling planet. It also lends humanist impulses to its Earthly subjects, and is certainly closely linked with the breakthrough works and revolutionary thinking of such eminent minds as Sigmund Freud, Charles Darwin and Isaac Newton.

Uranus is the first of the 'impersonal' planets and rules less intimate relationships such as friendships and acquaintanceships. It also denotes memberships of clubs, societies, groups and political organisations, and is associated with modern inventions such as electricity, computers, aviation, television, and the discovery of radiation. Concerned with the realm of ideas and the intellect, it exudes an air of coolness and logic. But most of all, this planet's role is to break down the established 'order' and replace it with experimental, novel or idealistic regimes - whether these are applied to the wider world, or in our personal lives. It acts to break up the crystallisation that Saturn has imposed, and stands for originality, shock, inspiration, dynamic self-expression, will and the ability to synthesise. It also acts to electrify, galvanise, vivify, awaken and mobilise, often working in a spasmodic, unexpected fashion, but highly effective as an agent of change nonetheless. It signifies unusual characters, inventors, electricians, and those with transcendental interests. Uranus is a political planet which seeks to change and manoeuvre the world into new ways of thinking and *being*.

Before the discovery of the three outer planets which lay beyond the detection of the naked eye, the ruler of Aquarius was Saturn. Today, after the discovery of Uranus, Saturn is regarded as Aquarius's secondary or traditional ruler. Indeed, very old astrology texts describe Aquarians in Saturnian terms, which seems odd to most now, given the Aquarian temperament is regarded as the polar opposite of everything traditional or Saturnian. Occasionally, however, you may still meet with an Aquarian who is cautious, conservative, even dull, slow-going, melancholy, quiet, thoughtful, deep, reticent and restrained in their passions; you may even be one of these types yourself! But more often than not, a typical Aquarian will have been endowed with all that is Uranian: unpredictable, convention-defying, unusual, occasionally shocking, different, eccentric and in extreme cases, that one oddball in the crowd we all know and love. It is Uranus's influence which helps make the Water Bearer the prophet, social reformer, brilliant thinker and free spirit that he doubtless is.

Uranus, the primal Greek God who ruled the sky and the personification of the Greek heaven, is brilliant and loves the original and the unconventional, whether it be astonishing invention or acts of wilful rebellion. In short, Uranus 'shakes it up'. Uranus is the 'rebel' and the 'outsider' and corresponds with our urge to break down constraints of the past; in the individual context, this can mean breaking old patterns of behaviour. On a collective level, but stemming from the individual, it signifies the urge for reform, revolution, change and the realisation of new ideas.

Uranus is associated with the abnormal, aircraft, astrology, brotherhood, electrical engineers, transformers, agitators, airports, divorce, alarms, homosexuality, anarchy, freaks, altruism, freedom, appliances, microphones, disorder, astronomy, stereograms, avant garde, aviation, the unexpected, batteries, bohemia, experiments, boycotts, changes, circulation, tornadoes, computers, shocks, spark plugs, contradictions, convulsions, cranks, informalities, peculiarities, aliens, prodigies, interruptions, discoveries, innovations, disruptions, turbines, twitching, unconventionality, dynamo, earthquakes, spasms, eccentricities, electricity, electronics, ankles, elopement, advanced ideas, erratic behaviours, exile, sonar, 'the uninvited', upheavals, upsets, extraordinary, flashes, sudden, foreign, fugitives, gales, elevators, hippies, impulses, independence, inventions, liberation, libertine, lightning, metaphysics, humanism, the new and modern, radar, strikes, radiators, nonconformists, strangeness, novelties, occultism, originality, outlaws, paradoxes, radicalism, radios, rebels, reform, generators, genius, helicopters, research, runaways, scientists, separations, surprises, switchboards, television, trespassing, hurricanes, and X-rays. I'm sure you get the idea!

Uranus, as one of the three outer or generational planets, is regarded as a 'planet of a higher octave', along with Neptune and Pluto. These higher octave forces account for those flashes of inspiration we are occasionally jolted with, when we become especially aware of our life's purpose, albeit usually only very fleetingly - unless of course you are an Aquarian!

Uranus embodies esoteric principles which symbolise vibrations of cosmic energy that affect whole generations and collective mankind, rather than touching us on a personal level; however, Aquarians and other people whose Uranus is strongly placed or emphasised in their birth chart, can certainly be individually affected by this planet's influence.

Uranus is Mercury's higher octave, and although both function on an intellectual level, Mercury rules the everyday and logic, while Uranus rules intuition and sees far further than the immediate moment and environment. It could also be said that Mercury is the trickster, Uranus the magician. Here, the versatile is raised to the volatile. In its elevated role, Uranus allows mortals to bring the beauty of knowledge and intellect to a more original, inventive and creative level, and in the birth chart, Uranus rules the higher mind, a planetary energy which helps one deal not only with what is but also with what can be. While Mercury is connected with the gathering and learning of information on a daily, mundane basis, Uranus rules the vast amounts of information accumulated over a long period of time, and are therefore manifested as intuition and sustained intelligence. If Mercury is the messenger, student, reporter and learner, Uranus is the sage, the wise teacher and the judge; Aquarians can see how fortunate they are to have such a powerful guardian planet, and must also assume the duty to use this power advantageously.

Uranus never seeks to put up boundaries around your soul or spirit, allowing you to more easily build and create things according to your own inner visions, ideals and views of the world. A legacy of your ruling planet, chaos to you is actually beneficial; in fact, it produces a bubbling, creative cauldron in which you can create the most useful, innovative and magical of things. Uranus also gives its Aquarian charges the tendency to need more change and serendipity in your life than other zodiac signs. Uranus teaches you that you have a bigger job to do and there is no time for sitting still, which suits you fine. Commotion is your forte, and when things get dull you deliberately shake them up by rattling the apple cart. In this way, Aquarians and Uranus work in very sudden and unexpected ways, which is why this planet is called the Great Awakener, and why its offspring are so rebellious.

Uranus is not content with leading the way along existing roads; instead, it will carve a new channel through the mountains where nobody thought roads could ever be created. Sometimes this road takes unexpected twists and turns; such is the nature of this unpredictable planet. But Uranus doesn't *make* us believe in magic, for that belief already exists within most of us, instead it reinforces our belief in it, by dropping moments of serendipity, dazzling insights or unexpected surprises into our laps. Uranus may pull rabbits out of the cosmic hat and enchant us with its inexplicable genius, but it is also capable of pulling the magical carpet out from under us just as suddenly, leaving us shocked and a little bewildered. Life - and Uranus - has a way of doing that.

Aquarians are said to be ahead of their time, and therefore slightly out of sync with the surrounding world. The Industrial Revolution, a historical period which followed the discovery of Uranus, ushered in the apparent Age of Enlightenment, or at least the Age of Technology. Ever since that period of time, it has been suggested that we are entering the cusp of the Age of Aquarius, and while we are not all the way into it yet, we are certainly in transition. Considering that an astrological age takes around 2,100 years to complete, the cusp can take a couple of hundred years. The reason the Age of Aquarius has been so glorified and embraced with mounting excitement, is that Uranus rules this sign. We can expect a Uranian rush of energy, thrills, adventure, progress, changes and above all, advancement. This planet has a tendency of sending us rushing off in all directions to find the gold at the end of the rainbow, which is yet to be found - but the pot of gold that the Age of Aquarius stands for is nearly upon us. In fact, Aquarians are already in firm possession of it, as they are living already in that rosy-coloured utopian future its profound influence promises us all.

In today's world, many Aquarian-themed ideas have emerged, and Aquarian technologies have brought about so much information that we can safely label our times the 'Age of Information'. Although we are not yet living in the Age of Aquarius, the concepts of the Water Bearer have been emerging more strongly as each new decade unfolds, and humanity is slowly making the great shift towards seeing each individual as a part of the whole. Uranus has a grand plan, an aspiration to roll out a new spiral of evolutionary accomplishment for humanity, and will indeed live it out through those upon whom it bestows the gift of effecting this whole-world change to - namely, Aquarians.

Uranus is the planet which embodies the sixth sense, and Aquarians are often gifted with the flashes of insight that are characteristic of the higher, spiritual faculties of the mind. Uranian individuals are therefore blessed with the futuristic and brilliant intellect that a strong Uranian influence implies, especially if at the time of your birth Uranus was well-placed in the sky in relation to Mercury, the two combining forces to indicate genius.

Revolutionary by nature, true Uranians are idealistic and work towards the betterment of humanity, never satisfied with past traditions or present 'realities'. Uranus can manifest in us individually as erratic rebellion or the inner peace of simply 'being' an individual. It indicates the launching of oneself or one's ideas into a new environment, taking the risk for change, and disconnection in order to be able to stand back and see more clearly. It signifies one's level of individuality, freedom, extremism, radicalism, reformist side, anarchism, fanaticism, electricity, inventiveness and unpredictability. It is concerned with the collective mind, illumination, awakening, unconventionality and new discoveries. It is the humanitarian urge, the great 'awakener' in social change and on a personal, individual level it can awaken our 'dormant' side, understanding things conceptually and with vision. Essentially uncomfortable with feelings, it has a detached understanding of the world. Uranus is what gives us sudden flashes of inspiration, ideas and thoughts, and signifies our instinctive understanding of what may be hidden and unseen, and of what is not known by the conscious mind.

Uranus, being the ruler of Aquarius, the sign which has long been associated with pouring forth from heaven the 'waters of life' onto humanity, lends a prophetic and futuristic slant to the Water Bearer's mind. However, the sheer force of Uranian creativity seldom reaches its pure 'cosmic' form, as pure creative power can cause turbulence and disturbance in the Earthly human psyche, and this turbulence usually manifests as acts of rebellion against the past, the 'establishment' and traditional structures rather than explosive revelation.

The Uranus influence upon the Aquarian soul urges the Water Bearer to enlighten others and certainly to pour the waters of knowledge onto his fellow humans, friend or foe. Not that Aquarians have many, or indeed any, enemies, for ignorance to these souls is not bliss but potential devastation. Being ever tolerant, they are rarely prejudiced and do not discriminate; there is more than enough water in their urn to soften and water the arid fields of ignorance and societal discord.

The Uranian character has a pioneering spirit and super consciousness that has often arrived after the sacrifice of an element of personal or Earthly life, and pure Uranian types have contributed significantly to the progressive and evolutionary process of life across the globe. Indeed, Uranus is the iconoclast and the divine rebel of the Solar system, and he drives the human will through his creative powers. In fact, according to mythology, he started out as a creator before he became the rebel of the skies.

The position of Uranus in your birth chart will tell you about your levels of social rebelliousness, but being an Aquarian, it's a pretty sure bet that this planet exerts a somewhat significant influence upon you regardless. Bohemianism (also a product of the spiritual Neptune), a yearning for freedom, and new age progressive thinking all form part of the typical Aquarian style; although you may not be socially rebellious, your urge for freedom may be expressed on an internal level rather than through lifestyle. As an inherent rebel, however, Uranus will ensure that your spirit will live according to its own rules, in whatever form of expression it manifests.

Being prominent in your psyche as Aquarius's modern ruling planet, Uranus gives you a heightened intellect, access to brilliant ideas and a sense of the unusual and 'different'. An original thinker with often lightning flash thoughts, you love the unpredictable side of life, sometimes revelling in chaos, upheavals or change, which is when you come into your own. You instinctively know how to handle crises and are able to keep a cool head about you when all around are losing theirs.

Uranus, along with Jupiter, is associated with lightning, and bestows the Aquarian with those lightning bolt thinking processes. However, these thoughts may never make it to Earth, and the sense of frustration that the soaring Aquarian spirit so often experiences, is due to its flying high among the nebulae, keenly aware of the Universal order of the cosmos, but trapped in an Earthly body that is typically restricted and tied up in chains. Those Uranian characters who are unable to find a way to reconcile this creative dilemma can often suffer isolation and loneliness, for when one has flown though or resided in the kingdoms of greatness, the real world beneath one's feet can be a very lonely place.

Uranian energy, magnetism and attraction is often at work in matters of love. Romantic adventures that begin under a strong Uranian influence often end as intensely and abruptly as they began. Aquarians need to guard against this erratic and unpredictable influence, which has a particularly strong effect upon their lives and characters. This is especially true during natal transitions to your ruling planet, when you may find yourself overwhelmingly drawn to someone's magnetic field or 'aura', only to be brought back down to Earth and reality once the transit is complete. These transit periods are often characterised by a feeling of being elevated to euphoric states and heavenly heights, but Uranus has a way of delivering the unexpected with its characteristic shock value.

A strong Uranus makes for a friendly, independent, kind, but rather detached and sometimes isolated character who possesses an inventive brain and a broad, far-seeing mind. However, you may also be obstinate and have a determination to live your life in your own way. Your unorthodox approach to situations and your embedded rebellious tendencies, however well-hidden or misunderstood by others, are usually used for the betterment of others' lives and the advancement of society in general, e.g. through invention and innovative ideas. You have a pure heart which is firmly in the right place, and are well-intentioned, especially when it comes to defending the 'underdog'. Above all, you seek and *live* the truth, despite your employing of unusual methods to capture its essence.

All significant Uranus aspects can have a profound effect upon our lives. It takes 84 years to fully return to the position it was in at the time of our birth. Therefore, approximately every 20 to 21 years, it will form a significant aspect to its natal position, with the first square aspect occurring at 21 years of age, when the spirit of rebellion and 'breaking free' is at its height. At around the age of 42, it forms an opposition to its natal position, and this is when we start to really assess and search ourselves to work out whether or not we have achieved our goals or realised our dreams. Wisdom may very well teach us that this is the time to shift the focus of our attention from purely material or worldly concerns, to more spiritual, creative and individuated goals, which is much more aligned with Uranus's nature. The final square occurs at the age of approximately 63, and significantly, this is around the age of retirement, a time to break free from the restrictions of working life and paying off a traditional mortgage or other material goals. Uranus returns to its own natal position when we are 84, usually the end of the life span - that's if we don't miss it altogether through death or dementia. These are the years when arguably truly magical things can happen for us. If we were to take a cue from native tribes who honour, respect and revere their elders, we may even experience the ultimate Uranian enlightenment of this phase of life, which we were destined to meet. Symbolically, this final Uranian infusion suggests a potential for spiritual re-birth, particularly for the Aquarian spirit, and a new adventure in detaching ourselves at last from the world altogether in order to fix our sights upon greener and freer horizons.

This Uranian energy and influence, throughout your whole life, gives Aquarians the 'gifts' of vision, originality, futuristic thinking, and eccentricity, giving the potential to be the impactful 'outsider', and the bringer of hope and messages society most needs to hear. Too much of this Uranian energy can make one anarchistic, fanatical, contrary, unpredictable, inflexible and overly eccentric, to the point of 'dropping out' of or being rejected by society. But the Aquarian always knows what's best for his own soul; after all, your motto is "I Know," because deep down, you really do *know*, even if you can never quite manage to articulate *what* it is exactly that you know. How will *you* use your phenomenally powerful Uranian influence?

★ A NOTE ON THE THREE OUTER OR DISTANT PLANETS ★
URANUS, NEPTUNE & PLUTO

It has been said that the distant planets are actually *more* powerful than the others as they take longer to orbit the Sun; they therefore affect whole generations of people rather than individuals. But as a result of their longer-spanning orbits, these slower moving planets (Uranus, Neptune and Pluto) dwell in the zodiac constellations for longer periods of time, allowing them to leave a deeper and more indelible experience on the human psyche and experience than the swifter moving planets. In other words, their effect is thought to be more lingering.

YOUR HOUSE IN THE HOROSCOPE ★ THE ELEVENTH HOUSE

The Eleventh House relates to society, to friendship and to groups you interact with regularly. It illustrates your hopes, wishes and aspirations on a more qualitative level than the aims and ambitions of the Tenth House before it.

A house is one of the twelve sections dividing the terrestrial globe, viewed from a precise time and geographical place, into sectors from the poles to the horizon. The horoscope, or birth chart, is divided into these twelve sections called houses. Each house governs a different area or 'department' of life, such as relationships, career, leisure and even karma. The reason for this division of the Earth into houses can be understood when we consider that the Sun's rays affect us differently in the morning, at noon and at night, and also in summer and winter, and if we study the cause, we will readily observe that it is the angle at which the ray strikes us or the Earth which produces that difference in effect. Similarly, with the stellar rays, astrologers have observed that a child born at or near midday, when the Sun's rays strike the birthplace from the Tenth House, has an improved chance of public or career advancement in life than one born after sunset. By similar observations and tabulations, it has been found that the other planetary rays affect the various departments of life when their ray is projected through the other houses, and therefore each house is said to 'rule' or govern certain departments of the human life experience.

The Eleventh House, ruled by Aquarius, is the house of friendships, acquaintanceships, groups, social life, group involvement, social affinities, clubs and organisations, collectives, networking, social conscience, social causes, progress, ideals, global awareness, progress, political visions, and our hopes, wishes and aspirations. It shows how you are able to get along with others as part of a group, and how altruistic you are in your outlook. Personal contacts on a far and wide, and more or less impersonal, scale, and the depth of one's involvement with humanitarian or social causes is also found here.

As an Air sign, this is one of the three Houses of Relationships. But where Gemini is concerned with relationships on a personal level and Libra on an interpersonal level, the Aquarius-ruled Eleventh House is concerned with relationships on a transpersonal, or wider-reaching, level.

This house tells us much about our social life and work associates. On a personal level, the eleventh sphere of the wheel also reveals how we pursue our ideals, hopes, dreams and aspirations, and gives us hints about how we can incorporate other people socially and within groups, to help us reach our highest goals and ideals, on both a personal and (more often) collective level. It also shows what we may achieve by tailoring our personal goals to the needs of society, and teaches us that the endeavours of a coordinated group can achieve more than the sum of several individual efforts. Planets in this house indicate the type of friends who attract us and where we find common interests with others.

This house is not concerned with self-gratification or personal pleasure like its opposite Leo's Fifth House is; instead it operates in an impersonal sphere of life, dealing with cerebral spirituality and global-realisation rather than self-actualisation.

In the Eleventh House we see how we integrate into the group; how we operate within the larger system. The traditional name for this house was in fact the House of Hopes, Dreams and Wishes. It can also be described as the realm of communal spirit, the House of Brotherhood, or the House of Friends and Idealism.

If the Eleventh House influence is strong in the birth chart, such as being born under an Aquarian Sun, we will be inclined to choose forms of self-expression which involve the group more so than the individual. The Eleventh House ensures that we pour out our precious waters of consciousness where they are needed the most: upon groups and societies, and the world at large. The global community, after all, is a perpetually thirsty place, ever in need of a refreshing drink.

YOUR OPPOSITE SIGN ★ LEO
WHAT YOU CAN LEARN FROM THE LION

If we look at the zodiac, we can see that it can be broadly divided into two hemispheres, this division being based on the natural division of the year by the two equinoxes. Astrologers often refer to the first six signs, the hemisphere in which the day predominates (the days being longer in the spring and summer months), as the Personal Sphere of Experience, and the second six signs, the hemisphere in which nights are longer, as the Social Sphere of Experience. These two halves of the zodiac perfectly balance and complement each other, and each individual 'personal' zodiac sign has something to teach its directly opposite 'social' zodiac sign. To generalise, the signs of the personal sphere tend to experience life through a type of self-projection and self-interest which is often socially uncomplicated, unsophisticated or naïve. Their objective is to learn greater social awareness and thereby integrate themselves with the larger, more Universal human collective. On the other hand, the signs of the social sphere are prone to experience life through the use of their more developed social consciousness. In essence, the personal signs (Aries, Taurus, Gemini, Cancer, Leo, Virgo) usually provide stimulation and new energy to their environment, while the social, more Universal signs (Libra, Scorpio, Sagittarius, Capricorn, Aquarius, Pisces) provide experience, opportunities for wider expression, and give a more broad-minded approach and perspective to their surroundings.

Each sign in a pair seeks and is attracted to the qualities of its complementary opposing sign. Leo seeks the social inclusiveness of Aquarius, while the Aquarius desires the sense of individuality, confidence and strength of purpose embodied by Leo. Leo dwells within the realm of the organisation and projection of individual ambitions and *personal* ideals and creativity, while Aquarius resides within the realm of the organisation and projection of social ambitions and *collective* ideals and contributions.

Positive and Fixed, the balance of this polarity is between the artist and the scientist, the individual and the group, the strong-ego and the absent-ego, the autocrat and the democrat. Leo is self-centred and radiates self-confidence like the Sun radiates warmth, while the pure Aquarian is only one cog in a vast operating system and is not motivated by self-interest or ambition. Leo can be an egotistical and arrogant dictator who may become oblivious to the existence of those 'beneath' him, unless they serve as exploitable followers. Aquarius looks after the rights of others he considers his 'brothers', ever upholding causes and personal ideals that work towards the benefit of all. The Leo can be so intent on furthering his individual ego-based creativity, that he can easily lose sight of other people; through over-emphasising his own needs, he tends to neglect others and as a result, disregards their input. To help overcome this undesirable trait, he can look towards the group-oriented approach of Aquarius for support.

Although the word 'opposite' conjures up feelings of separateness and differences, the astrological polarities should not be seen as two signs in conflict with each other - their positive expression is to create a natural balance and equilibrium. Each sign has something to learn from its opposite, but also has a contribution to make towards the other sign's more evolved expression. The Fifth (Leo) and the Eleventh (Aquarius) House polarity is concerned with personal creativity versus group creativity and contribution.

The modern associations between Aquarius and Uranus has given this sign an often exaggerated reputation for being rebellious, difficult, eccentric, perverse and unstable. All of these negative traits and behaviours arise as extreme manifestations in individuals who have not yet found their centre - or their heart. This is Leo's domain, and from this very centre it can teach a lot to its Water Bearer friends.

The two houses ruled by Leo and Aquarius in the horoscope are the Fifth and Eleventh houses. The Fifth House is where a person consolidates and expresses his individuality and outer identity through various leisurely and creative pleasures, whereas the eleventh house is a less personal, more widely varying expression of one's individuality - usually concerning the individual in the context of a group or wider society. It indicates one's altruistic attitudes and activities, friendships, social connections and broad motivations and aspirations, while the opposing Fifth House is much more individually-centred and self-oriented.

Although the Sun is in detriment in the sign of Aquarius (being opposite Leo, which is ruled by the Sun), the Water Bearer will usually still manage to make their mark on the world, albeit in a less 'showy' way than their Lion opposite. Nonetheless, being in detriment, the Sun is quite weak in the sign of the Water Bearer, and Aquarians may feel at times (or all of the time) lacking in self-confidence and unsure of themselves, and shun the limelight. You may also suffer a weak or ineffective ego, and find it difficult to assert yourself and truly 'shine' or stand tall and proud. These are Leo's forte; the Lion can certainly teach you lessons in straightening your back, lifting your chin up and looking upwards to the Sun.

Aquarius is primarily an impersonal and group-oriented sign, and operates according to thinking principles. It is concerned with the energies of the group rather than with the personal creative unfolding of the individual. Leo is individualistic and uninterested in the group; it seeks above all to become what it envisions as its own heroic potential. Aquarius is logical, consistent and principled; Leo is dramatic, spontaneous, intuitive and seeks myth rather than fact. Aquarius believes the 'whole' is more important than the parts which compose it, seeking hard facts, logical principles and behaves with the benefit of the collective or the 'group' in mind; Leo seeks joy, self-expression, spontaneity, the right to believe in magic and to bring fairy tales alive on life's vast stage. Aquarius, on the other hand, with its innately broader viewpoint, will promptly wipe out the individual if it runs too rampant in life's theatre.

The creative individual, intent on developing his own uniqueness and creative power (Leo), seeks to become aware of the larger human family of which he is a part, so that he may offer his creative gifts with an objective understanding of their value to others (Aquarius). Aquarius, being a group-conscious individual, is aware of the importance of the needs of others around him, but needs to develop a stronger ego, true self-confidence, a greater sense of his own value and creativity so that he has something of his own to offer, which is the energy he can learn from Leo.

To evolve to your fullest potential, you need to learn the Lion's lessons of expressing your life force creatively from deep within your heart and thus empower your soul. Your karmic goal is to become heart-centred and empowered. In order to develop your true highest potential and follow your soul's true path, your soul needs to learn how to give and receive affection more freely, allow your natural warmth to shine through and trust in your heart rather than your head. Aquarians tend to rely mostly on their intellectual reasoning to make decisions when they've reached a crossroads, and are often in need of some hearty lessons from the Lion.

Being an Aquarian, you may also behave in a way that is self-preserving or protective of yourself, as you are afraid your ideas may not be accepted, but if you work on emanating warmth to others and swallowing your intellectual pride, you will be more open to receiving love and abundance in all its forms. You also need to work on being more assertive and expressive and a little bit more 'bossy' than you may feel comfortable with. Taking the lead and being in the limelight may feel awkward for you as it is not something the Aquarian soul is well acquainted with, but once you are a bit more practised in these areas, your life's journey will reflect back to you, greater success and stronger meaning.

Your creative talents need to be tapped into to allow the real *you* to flow more naturally through life. Having suppressed these creative outlets in the past, perhaps thinking that they are not rational, you have put your mind before your true instincts, which are telling you to flower into a more creative and outwardly expressive person.

Typical of Aquarius, periods of low self-esteem and a weak ego have likely been a huge hindrance for you so far on your life's path, so it would be really helpful for you to learn some self-confidence which will transform your life with amazing results. Being outwardly expressive and demonstrative may be difficult for you in the beginning, but your soul's inner voice is telling you that these need working on. Leo is sitting across the astrological table from you, and this generous, giving spirit will happily provide the light you need for the heart-centred path ahead.

Leo can teach you the value of relating to children, romance, play time, affection, leisure, relaxing, a willingness to take risks, and indulging in personal pleasures. They can also encourage in you a greater desire to express yourself creatively, to channel your creative energies more effectively, and to play with and nurture your inner child more often.

Ultimately, you need to come out of your shell and announce your arrival to the world, in true Leo style! And you can be guaranteed that as you come out from behind those curtains, somewhere in the audience, one very proud Lion, symbolically or real, will be the first to applaud your grand entrance. The whole pride might even attend your opening night if you're super lucky.

WHAT THE LION CAN ULTIMATELY TEACH THE WATER BEARER

Release ★ Detachment, modesty, shyness, unpredictable behaviour, off-handedness, coolness, aloofness, lack of confidence, scattered thoughts, eccentricity, perversity

Embrace ★ Warmth, self-confidence, pride, affection, individual focus, ego-examination, willpower, courage, nobility of spirit, generosity, vitality, power, leadership, genuine leisure and pleasure, stronger ego, personal creativity, more emphasis on the heart than the head

The Leonine spirit lives with pure heart. You are naturally independent and paradoxical, which can be endearing and intriguing, but also alienating. You often stand out because of your outspoken manner, offhandedness and your acute sense of friendships and relationships. Although you retain your personal freedom, you often show yourself as excessively available to others, an attitude which hides a deep need for the comfort, warmth and security that you so lack. You also lack courage and willpower, but Leo the Lion is more than generous in teaching you how you can acquire these and much, much more - even if the sole reason he is imparting his feline wisdom *is* to advance his own ego.

MAGIC, DRAWING, ATTRACTION, SPELLS, RITUALS, WISHING & POWER

A Note on the Universe

Within each of us resides the merging of the Sun and the Moon, the dance of the constellations, the vibrations of the planets, and the vast microcosm and macrocosm of the entire *Universe*. Uni means 'one' and Verse means 'song'; therefore, the word Universe literally means 'One Song'. If you learn to tune yourself in, you can even hear it!

What is Magic?

Magic is a kind of special energy that is beyond description, and like most kinds of energy it has its own rules and ways of being manipulated. It remains an elusive term, and no definition has ever really found Universal acceptance. Attempts to separate it from superstition, religion and other-worldly phenomena on the one hand, and 'science' on the other, are ridden with difficulties. However slippery the term 'magic' might be, there is a general agreement that most of us wish for more of its presence in our lives and often fall short of achieving this wish.

Those performing spells, 'asking the Universe', wishing, praying, or undertaking rituals, are using this very special energy to draw things to them. Learning to manipulate energy in these ways is never hard (and shouldn't be), but it can be complex and does require knowledge, practice, creativity, patience and above all, imagination. Most of us use simple magic every day, whether by saying little prayers, making wishes, visualising, and exchanging - sending out and receiving - good, positive or hopeful vibes. When you understand that all the forces and magic you need are *within* you, and you learn to *believe* in that power, you are then able to make all manner of changes to your life and, most importantly, yourself.

Magic is an invisible force which connects and permeates everything. Every thought you have and every action you take, will affect the strength of this force, and can be influenced and directed towards a specific purpose by using certain means. The most important of these are your intentions, facing in the direction of your desired outcome, your will and your *belief* that it works. The more you want something to happen, and the clearer you can visualise the desired outcome, the stronger your will and feelings towards it will be, ensuring an avalanche of amazing people, events and circumstances will flow into your experiences, gathering speed, momentum and power as it nears your goal or dream.

The Universe (or whichever higher power you believe in) works for us and through us. Ideas are given to us but they must be carried out *through* us, in the form of asking or acting or performing a ritual or casting a specific spell. The Universe's abundance is your abundance, and it flows through your mind into manifestation. The Universe or Divine Being in which you believe, gives you the necessary ideas and clothes them with all that is needed to bring them into form when we ask *believing*.

Based on ancient human beliefs, systems and superstitions, declaring what you want and acting out your deepest desires can actually help to make things happen. Magical ideas include the notion that thought affects matter and that the trained imagination can alter the physical world, that all aspects of the Universe are interdependent and that we can discover connections and correspondences between everyday occurrences and cosmic, or Divine, energies. A miracle or a wish coming true can suggest something is going on that extends beyond the laws of nature, that something unseen has occurred; but just because we cannot see it or touch it, it doesn't mean it's not there. Magic exists, especially if you truly believe it does, but science is so far incapable of capturing its essence or the rationale behind it. Personally, I prefer to leave that task to the higher powers of the Universe.

To help your dreams come true and to use your inborn power to its full effect, you can employ boosters based on the special energies and qualities of your Sun sign. These 'boosters' are chosen to be in alignment with the purpose of a particular goal, and contain energies of their own which will enhance the strength of your spell, prayer, ritual or 'asking'. Specific magical energies can be invoked by carrying out a spell or ceremony using specific herbs or colours, or on a particular day of the week, according to either your Sun sign (to heighten the power of the asking), and/or that is in sympathy with that for which you are asking (I have included days of the week for other Sun signs and spell types).

Some materials and boosters you can use to increase the power, magic or energy in any area of your life include: candles, wish lists (written on an appropriate piece of paper written with a specially-chosen writing tool), symbols, affirmations, chants, incense, herbs and flowers, locations, colours, days of the week, elements, crystals and gemstones, animal symbols, charms, talismans, amulets, gods and goddesses, essential oils, planetary hours and your Solar totem animals. All are covered, some more briefly than others, for your very special Sun sign to radiate the energy to powerfully draw your wildest dreams towards you!

Overall, it pays to remember that the Universe (or whatever higher power/s or force/s you happen to believe in) creates *through* you that to which you give your attention. What you contemplate becomes the law of your being, and through your pure unwavering belief, is eventually brought through to manifestation on the material plane. What you think about is entirely up to you. But just be mindful that whatever you think about the most becomes your dominant thought, then your main point of attraction, and is ultimately magnified until it becomes your reality or your experience. So choose your thoughts with care. And to quote Ralph Waldo Emerson, "Be careful what you set your heart upon, for it will surely be yours." I carry a copy of this beautiful prophecy in my purse as its words resonate so strongly with me. In other words, be mindful about what you're wishing for, for you will most probably get it, whether it's good or bad - magic, after all, doesn't discriminate. Just make your dominant thoughts good ones, and you will attract everything you set your heart and intentions upon. Good luck!

ASTROLOGY & MAGIC

"Everyone practices magic, whether they realise it or not, for magic is the art of attracting particular influences, events and situations within human life. Magic is a natural phenomenon because the Universe is reflexive, responding to human thoughts, aspirations and desires ..."
David Fideler, *Jesus Christ, Sun of God*

Astrology is the most sublime of the occult * sciences, while at the same time it is one of the most practical for everyday application, for it divines the human soul itself. The cosmos, particularly the patterns that formed across it at the exact moment we were born, indicates the road along which our mental and spiritual endowments are likely to impel us, therefore enabling us to prepare in advance for life's battles, pitfalls, milestones, celebrations and of course to make the utmost of opportunities. Such is the magic of the human mind, that it can 'see' into the future and relive the past without having to be physically present in either, and when combined with astrological *knowing*, particularly the knowing that springs from understanding some of the dynamics of our natal chart, however basic, our inner - and outer - magic can be lifted to phenomenal heights.

In ancient times, not only was astrology the ardent study of the most learned and powerful minds, but among the masses of ordinary people its authority and guidance was accepted and followed without question. How this powerful knowledge was used was - and still is - up to the individual, but all who used it applied it to their perceived advantage.

As primitive humans observed the skies, no doubt they gradually realised that certain stars upon which their fate depended accompanied the seasons, or certain times of the year. They may also have reasoned that if governed their fate, they also governed their bodies, and it is therefore conceivable that the skies were associated with Divine influence. Certain celestial influences were believed to emanate from the thirty-six decans of the signs, and the mysterious but apparent effect that they exercised upon humans were thought to be due to a subtle ether shed by the heavenly stars and spheres on the Earth, that affected not only people, but also other animals, plants and minerals. For the ancient mind, linking magic with astrology may have also provided a much needed sense of predictability and patterns.

Early astrologers named and made associations with the imaginary divisions of the twelve signs and the twelve houses, and people born under a certain sign were said to inherit to an extent, its properties and nature. They also believed that the influence of the planets and stars corresponded with the medicinal properties of certain plants and minerals. They therefore asserted that the influence of a star or planetary position would affect the type of medicine or healing they would offer a subject to attain the most beneficial outcome. Throughout the writings of early philosophers and theorists, there is constant reference to this unmistakable mystic connection between the seven known planets and Earthly affairs and ailments. The seven metals were connected with the seven planets, to which the seven colours and the seven transformations were added. So the alchemist came to share the astrological doctrine that each planet ruled some mineral: The Sun ruled gold, the Moon silver, Mars iron, Venus copper, Saturn lead, Jupiter tin, and Mercury quicksilver. Consequently, in alchemical symbolism the same sign came to represent the metal and its corresponding planet.

In subsequent years, astrology became closely related to alchemical knowledge and development, and the alchemist came to be regarded as an authority not only on the transmutation of metals, but also on astrology and magic. This goes some of the way to explaining how magic and divination, which had always been inseparably bound up with astrology, came to be associated with alchemy. In all the occult sciences, the supreme power was believed to be in the stars above, and from their mysterious emanations all the metals, crystals, minerals, plants and herbs derived their special properties over time. Further, as alchemy became ever more spiritual and concerned with more abstract and philosophical concepts, eventually it was considered that the transmutation of lead into gold was simply a metaphor for the transformation of base matter, in this case the human soul, into a much purer and higher state of wisdom and being.

The Sun and Moon were believed to have greater influence over the human body than all the other heavenly bodies, and to exert their influence in various ways whenever they entered a certain sign of the zodiac. And although the Moon was traditionally regarded as the most important factor of a horoscope, the Sun has come into its own in later centuries, with the result that almost everyone knows their Sun sign but only those who have delved deeper are aware of the sign their natal Moon falls in. For this reason, I have chosen to focus this book series on the twelve Sun signs, as this is what the majority of people are most familiar with.

The following pages contain methods, energies, materials and objects which may be used to increase the magic and power of your Sun sign's influence upon you. Precious stones, flowers, colours and so on, are regarded as having a potent effect upon good fortune by attuning your mind to receive harmonious vibrations from the astral forces that surround you.

Finally, a basic working knowledge of basic astronomy and astrology is an asset when working with luck, abundance, wealth and personal power. You can attract more of these things when you align yourself with the workings of the wider Universe, the movement of the Sun, stars, Moon and planets and become aware of the correlations between the outer cycles of the skies and the inner cycles within yourself. Also, for those who are knowledgeable about Moon phases, equinoxes and solstices, a world of lucky possibilities can also magically open up to you. You don't need to know about astrology's deepest complexities to understand how everything interrelates; just learning the basics will give you an edge - and hopefully the following lucky tips will provide you with at least a small glimpse into the insights gleaned from your Sun sign, which I am certain will endow upon you the potential for amazing results to manifest in your life - and maybe even a step up one further rung towards the heavens!

* The word 'occult' comes from the Latin *occultus*, which literally means 'knowledge of the hidden'.

USING COLOURS, CRYSTALS, DEITIES, PLANTS, FOODS & MATERIA SUBSTANCES FOR INCREASING POWER & MAGNETISING MAGIC

Alchemist, reformer and mystic Henry Cornelius Agrippa, born in 1486, in his principal work, *On Occult Philosophy*, expressed his belief in the doctrines of astrology and in the theory that the spirit of the world exists in the body of the world, just as the human spirit exists in the body of man. He contended that this spirit also abounds in the celestial bodies and descends in the rays of stars, so that the things influenced by their rays become conformable to them. By this spirit every occult property is conveyed into metals, stones, herbs and animals, through the Sun, Moon and planets, and even through the stars beyond and higher than the planets. A firm believer in the efficacy of charms, he stated that they may "be worn on the body bound to any part of it or hung around the neck, changing sickness into health or health into sickness." I believe the same effect could be applied to wishing and the thinking of positive thoughts, to mean, "Changing thoughts and dreams into manifest reality." He also recommended that these charms be worn in the form of finger rings (that have been created using the materials in agreement and harmony with your Sun Sign's magical energy).

Material substances are connected with abstract purposes by a complex but highly usable and accessible system of correspondences. Use these time-honoured connections in your own spells and wishes to magnetise your desires to you. The following pages will give you some materials, energies, forces and ideas you can summon the power of in order to enhance your magic and luck.

PLANETS

The Planetary influence of the day is important when 'asking' for something. If you are wishing for luck, for example, try working with your Sun sign's inherent energies combined with the perfect day of the week for it. So an Aquarian might try using his natural intellect and articulate expression, to ask for greater luck on a Thursday, which is Jupiter's Day and Jupiter is renowned for being a lucky planet, or better still, ask for luck on a Saturday, which is Saturn's Day, traditional planetary ruler of Aquarius, at the time of day when Jupiter's influence is at its most powerful (information about planetary hours for each day of the week can be found on the Internet or in books on the subject, and can be complex and detailed. It is an art to memorise the correct times, days and energies for the correct spells. If you are determined enough to achieve your dream or goal however, you will be determined enough to put in the research to do it properly!) Here is a very simplified list of the days of the week and their meanings:

DAYS OF THE WEEK & THEIR POWERS

MONDAY ★ Moon
Cancer

The Divine feminine, changes, intuition, emotions, secrets, dealing with women, purity, goodness, perfection, unity, psychic ability, magic, spirituality, invoking a goddess's or angel's guidance, anything that fluctuates, contracts, increases or decreases.

TUESDAY ★ Mars
Aries & Scorpio

Enthusiasm, competition, passion, energy, courage, protection, victory, anything requiring assertiveness, standing up for yourself, or a 'fighting spirit', determination, vitality, sexuality, self-confidence, men's power, men's mysteries, drive, ambition, achievement, triumph, masculinity.

WEDNESDAY ★ Mercury
Gemini & Virgo

Education, travel, exams, study, communication, making connections, thinking, dealing with siblings, writing and speaking, knowledge, learning, adaptability, charm, youth, absorbing information.

THURSDAY ★ Jupiter
Sagittarius & Pisces

Increase and expansion of anything (remember to be careful what you wish for), luck, growth, influence, worldly power, accomplishment, fulfilment, gambling, philosophy, higher education, abundance, optimism.

FRIDAY ★ Venus
Taurus & Libra

Love, luxury, the arts, indulgence, beauty, marriage, money, prosperity, fertility, women's power, women's mysteries, grace, charm, appeal, hope, pleasure, decorating, self-worth, self-esteem, personal values, business partnerships, romance, creativity, sharing, bonding.

SATURDAY ★ Saturn
Capricorn & Aquarius

Long-term goals, career, institutions, establishments, security, investments, karma, reversal, structure, protection, solitude, privacy, determination, ending, blocking, renewing, transforming, anything to do with the public.

SUNDAY ★ Sun
Leo

All-purpose, success, wishes, generosity, happiness, optimism, spirit/essence, recognition, health, vitality, material wealth, invoking a god's aid or guidance, personal empowerment, spirituality, the Divine masculine.

YOUR NATAL MOON PHASE

Although this book is aimed at enhancing your life through the energy of your Sun sign, a bit of Lunar help can give your wishing a boost! As well as using the planetary days and hours system to add a bit of zest to your wish fulfilment, try combining your Sun sign's power periods with your natal Moon phase (your natal Moon phase can be calculated using a number of sources on the internet, or through an astrologer), or even studying which constellation the Moon is situated in at certain times, to increase the power of your spells and asking rituals. For example, you might like to 'ask' for a promotion at work during a New/Waxing Moon period, particularly if the Moon happens to fall under an auspicious sign for career advancement, such as Capricorn. Your natal Moon phase can also be used to similar effect, by researching when your Moon phase will coincide with a certain Lunar constellation position.

In most astrological interpretations the Sun is regarded as the most important, central feature of a natal chart. But to many the Moon is equally, if not more, important than the Sun sign. Many ancient cultures considered the Moon sign to be more significant. The Moon passes through the 12 signs about every 2.5 days, usually covering the whole zodiac in around 27.3 days. The Moon symbolises our inner world, the world of feeling, emotions, habitual responses, instincts, intuition, security and the subconscious. It describes our nurturing style and needs, our emotional response to life, our attitudes and likely reactions to others, our instinctive responses, the receptive feminine side of ourselves, our experience of our mother or mother figure, and our childhood experience. It represents the soul. In relationships it symbolises how we like to be nurtured and cared for, and the potential depth of our involvement on personal intimate levels.

For many centuries, people across the world have recognised that the Moon influences the affairs of all living things on planet Earth. The waxing Moon appears to have a drawing, increasing and enhancing effect, whereas the waning Moon has a decreasing, receding and withdrawing effect. All things that come into being are stamped with the qualities of the prevailing Moon stage. It seems that people born during certain Lunar phases tend to share specific attributes with other people born during this same phase. In turn, their attributes will be subtly different from those of individuals born during any of the other stages in the Moon cycle. Knowing exactly which phase of the Moon you were born under gives you all kinds of extraordinarily valuable insights into your character, emotions, behaviour and motivations in life. It can make you aware of your deepest underlying drives, the fundamental purpose that you are drawn towards in life and the contribution you can make to others and society during the course of your lifetime. This knowledge may enable you to intuit and make the most of your own personal cyclical pattern that you go through each month, and allow you to know when the most auspicious periods of time are for you and your affairs, nurture yourself and channel your energies in the most positive directions.

Because this Lunar pattern repeats itself every month, you will find that you can even pace yourself on a long-term basis. This will enable you to effectively target your efforts and goals on periods of time that you know will be potentially fortunate for you. You may in fact find that your birth phase corresponds with the days of the month when you have abundant energy, feel inspired and can generate new ideas with ease. During this period, you should work towards the fruition of your efforts, bring your dreams into light and reach for the stars!

The Lunar Phases Are:

★ New Moon
★ First/Waxing Crescent
★ First Quarter
★ Waxing Gibbous Moon
★ Full Moon
★ Waning Gibbous / Disseminating Moon
★ Last Quarter
★ Waning Crescent / Balsamic Moon
★ Back to the New Moon

SPELLS, MAGIC & WISHING WITH MOON PHASES

Though the Moon has eight astronomical phases, it is the three phases corresponding to maiden, mother and crone that are the most significant in spells, ritual, wish magic and psychic work. By tuning into the physical Moon we can understand and harness these distinct energy phases in our daily lives and magical worlds. The four primary Lunar phases are the New Moon, First Quarter, Full Moon and the Last Quarter. Depending on what sort of spell you wish to perform, your spell should take place during one of these cycles or time periods. Each phase of the Moon is good for some types of magic, but not so much for others.

NEW MOON, WAXING & FIRST QUARTER

In astronomical terms, the New Moon occurs when the Moon rises and sets at the same time as the Sun. Both bodies are found in the same position compared with the Earth. Therefore, a Solar eclipse can only ever occur at the New Moon, when the two luminaries are found, for a short time, in a perfect line relative to the Earth, with the Moon positioned between the Sun and the Earth. The New Moon's sunlit face is hidden from the Earth.

In astrological terms, the New Moon occurs at a time when the Sun and the Moon are found in the same degree of the zodiac and therefore occupy the same zodiac sign, forming a conjunction, or a 'fusing' of energies.

In astronomical terms, the First Quarter occurs seven days after the New Moon. Seen from the Earth, this phase makes the Moon like a crescent, forming the shape of a capital D.

In astrological terms, it occurs when the Sun and the Moon form a ninety-degree angle, or the square aspect, inside the zodiac, the Moon always preceding the Sun.

As the New Moon marks the beginning of a new cycle, it symbolises fresh starts. This is an exceptional time to work magic and make wishes for new beginnings, and for the conception and initiation of new projects. Use this Moon phase for improving health, the gradual increase of prosperity, attracting good luck, fertility magic, finding new love, friendship or romance, job hunting, making plans for the future and increasing your general spiritual or psychic awareness.

Overall, the Waxing Crescent and First Quarter Moon phases are appropriate for spells, rituals and workings that involve growth, healing and increase. This is a period of time lasting approximately two weeks, to draw things toward you and increase things, such as love, prosperity and new opportunities. During this period is the time to bless new projects, anything that requires energy to grow, such as gardens, business ventures, new homes, or educational pursuits. Personal growth and healing are accented, as is 'attraction magic' - drawing something to you such as love, abundance, health, success or a new path - and if done well, you can expect results by the next Full Moon. Magical workings for gain, increase or bringing things to you should be initiated when the Moon is waxing (or New, going from Dark to Full). A time for divination of all kinds, spells of spiritual intention, and for any creative project you wish to see birthed, with magical and fruitful results.

While making a wish within the first forty-eight hours after the New Moon is a powerful way of helping it come to fruition, the most potent time for making wishes is actually within the first eight hours of the exact time of its position. Write down your wish list within this first eight hours on a piece of appropriately coloured paper with a special writing tool, and be sure to capture the essence of your wish by wording it in a way that charges your emotions and simply feels 'right'. Make a maximum of ten wishes (less is perfectly fine too), as making too many wishes might disperse their energy too much to be effective. After writing down your list and releasing your wishes to the Universe in whichever form you feel happy with, keep your list and check on it in a few days', weeks' or months' time to assess whether anything has shifted in the direction of your listed dreams, desires or goals. I'll bet it has - or at the very least, something even better has arrived in its place!

Although the first forty-eight hours after the New Moon is the most potent time to make a special wish, you can begin Waxing Moon magic when you can see the crescent in the sky and continue until the day before the Full Moon. The closer to the Full Moon, the more intense the energies. In fact, a personally devised ritual using any special Lunar-associated materials over three days up to and including the Full Moon is excellent for something you require urgently or within a short timeframe.

In some cultures, people turn over silver coins or jewellery three times when the crescent Moon appears in the sky and make a wish. As the Moon grows, it is believed that prosperity and good fortune will grow too.

While the New Moon is not known as a time for 'banishing' or releasing things we no longer want in our lives, I feel that if we are to ask and wish for things, we need to make room to receive them. Making room means that the Universe can slot it right into our lives where we have cleared our paths for it. Clutter, unwanted things, unhappy relationships, possessions that no longer serve us, are all things we can banish. So, to help what you are asking for come into your life quicker, the New Moon is a particularly opportune time to throw a few things out so you can make way for the new and clear up some space for that which you are wishing for. What are you waiting for? Start creating a space for your wishes today!

FULL MOON

In astronomical terms, the Full Moon occurs 14 days after the New Moon, on the day when the Moon sets at the same time the Sun rises, or conversely. The two luminaries are effectively facing each other, with the Earth in between, the Sun shining its light onto the reflective Moon, giving it the fully lit up appearance of a giant, bright, perfectly round sphere. Indeed, its entire face is bathed in sunlight. A Lunar eclipse can only occur at the Full Moon, when the Sun, Moon and Earth are all in line, and the Earth hides the lit side of the Moon to us.

In astrological terms, a Full Moon occurs at the time when the Sun and Moon are 180 degrees apart inside the zodiac, and therefore positioned in opposite signs, forming an opposition aspect.

The highest energy occurs at the Full Moon, making this is a powerful time for all manner of magical workings. Use the Full Moon phase for any immediate need, a sudden boost of power or courage, psychic protection, a change of career or location, travel, healing acute health conditions, the consummation of love or a commitment, justice, ambition and promotion of all kinds. This phase lasts approximately 3 days - 24 hours before the exact Full Moon, the day of, and 24 hours after it, according to many sources - giving us 3 full days to perform our spells. However, we are not strictly limited to a three-day period; the power of this phase can actually be accessed for seven days - three days prior to, the night of, and the three days after the Full Moon. The Full Moon period is when the Moon is at her most powerful, being the most luminous and radiant part of the cycle. Known as the 'high tide' of psychic power, the Full Moon represents culmination, climax, fulfilment and abundance. The Full Moon governs all kinds of magic, including manifestation, banishing, and is particularly good for calling forth protection and heightening your intuitive abilities. The Full Moon contains magic that calls forth personal power, fertility, spiritual development, and psychic awareness. Cleansing of ritual tools, crystals, wish lists, Tarot decks, and the like can be done during this phase. Magic worked during the Full Moon often takes one complete cycle to come to fruition. Try also reaffirming your desires during the New Moon to give them an added nudge in the right direction.

LAST QUARTER OR WANING MOON

In astronomical terms, the Last Quarter, or Waning Moon, occurs twenty-one days after the New Moon. The time difference between the rising and setting of the two luminaries is reduced to what it was at the First Quarter. Viewed from the Earth, the Moon resembles a crescent whose lit up area is decreasing in size, forming the shape of a capital C.

In astrological terms, the Waning Moon occurs when the Sun and Moon are positioned at ninety degree angles of each other in the zodiac, forming the square aspect again. However, during this phase, the Sun is instead *ahead* of the Moon.

The Waning Moon represents the Lunar cycle from Full to Dark. Any spells and magic performed during this period is based purely around banishing and releasing. It could involve releasing things which no longer serve you (such as behaviours, material things, relationships and attitudes), banishing negative energies, and removing obstacles which are standing in the way of achieving your goals or dreams. The Waning Moon is the best time for cleansing, gently releasing, eliminating, expelling and completion. It is of great assistance when you are wanting to let go of something, or someone, gradually. The Dark of the Moon, the period when the Moon is no longer visible to the naked eye, until the New Moon, is the most useful time for divination of all kinds.

★ What is your natal Moon phase type?
Can you think of ways you can combine it with the power of your Sun sign to effect change and bring about wonderful happenings? ★

HARNESSING YOUR PERSONAL MOON MAGIC ★ MOON IN AQUARIUS

When the Moon is in your sign of Aquarius, it is a great time for working magic around: Original and progressive ideas, innovation, heightened perception, idealism, independence, Universal love, reformation, revolutions, resourcefulness, individualism, and humanitarian pursuits. Suggested operations could be around rituals and spells to enhance inventiveness, finding new perspectives and ways to look at the world, challenging structures, institutions and the establishment, and questioning the status quo. Invoke the Lunar Aquarius for tapping into your visions, humanitarian projects, and for emotionally detaching yourself from a troublesome situation. It is also an opportune time to tap into your inner genius, and finding and defining yourself as an individual. As Aquarius is associated with the unusual and the intellectual, with the Moon here, it is a fantastic time for learning mathematics, science, the divinatory arts, or astrology.

THE MOON ★ WHAT IT REPRESENTS IN THE HUMAN PSYCHE & NATAL CHART

The Moon in the sky shines with the reflected light of the Sun. Although not a planet, the Moon is our nearest celestial neighbour and exerts a great influence upon us. The gravitational pull of the Moon affects our body fluids, which contribute to about 90 per cent of our biological make-up. It moves at approximately half a degree per hour and takes an average of 27.3 days to pass through all twelve zodiac signs, staying in each for around 2.5 days.

In astrology the Moon corresponds with the way in which we reflect and respond to what is going on around us. It has to do with our feelings, emotions and instincts and, in the same way the Moon influences the tides on planet Earth, it symbolises the ebb and flow of our emotional nature, our moods, fluctuations and changeability. The Moon is the archetype of the Mother, which is within us all, and represents the primary feminine principle in the natal chart. It is through the Moon that we express our parental instincts - caring, nurturing, protecting, sensitivity. The Moon has links with the past and the subconscious and it is from this almost primitive source that our natural instinctual forces flow.

The Moon is essentially a feminine principle and associates with the inner personality, receptivity, passivity and inward-oriented feelings. It can act as an inner guide to the deeper self, the unconscious self, figures half-shrouded in mystery, linking the hidden personal world of the subconscious to the clearer world of personal awareness.

The Moon is the innermost core of our being, private feelings, habitual reactions and subconscious habits. It is the caring, nurturing sustainer of life, the 'mother' of the zodiac. It tells us about how we seek security, our urge to nurture, our nurturing style, our responses and feelings and moods. The innermost core of our being, private feelings, subconscious habits. It is concerned with habits, mothering, habitual/instinctive responses and personality. It is our karma, our soul, our past.

The Moon represents our mother or mother figure, our feminine side, maternal instinct, our nurturing style and needs, our unconscious self, our emotional reactions, the subconscious, our feelings, instincts, intuition, receptivity, habits, what we need to feel secure, fluctuations, cycles, moods, and our childhood. Its position in the birth chart is very significant, because as well as revealing feminine qualities and the potential gentleness and tenderness of a being, the Moon also reveals important information about the experiences and expression of the five senses.

The Moon is essentially receptive and passive; it reflects the life experience rather than initiating it. Fluctuating and cyclical, the Moon is the planet (although technically a satellite) of the childhood experience, and instinctual reactions. It represents the mother (a child's experience and expectations of their mother), maternal instincts and the feminine principle, indicating how strongly these manifest in an individual, male or female.

As it represents what our childhood experience is likely to be, and childhood is essentially a time where our consciousness has not yet fully developed, our Moon sign traits seem to be more apparent in our younger years. We will usually show our Moon sign traits more so than our Sun sign traits during this developing period of infancy and early childhood, until we have the presence of mind to more consciously develop our ego and true core self (the Sun).

The symbol for the Moon ☽ is a representation of its crescent in its waxing phase from new to full, but it can also be seen as two half circles - these form a bowl shape, a receptacle, a feminine container that 'receives' and 'holds' anything put into it. The half circle, unlike the full circle of the Sun, is finite and incomplete, almost as if striving for wholeness.

The Moon represents our *soul*.

YOUR MOON SIGN

The Sun / Moon Polarity
Conscious & Unconscious, Night & Day, Yin & Yang

"Man does, woman is."
Edward Edinger

Your Moon Sign, representing your soul, and your Sun sign, representing your spirit, work together to form the foundation of your basic personality, expression and nature. If you know what your Moon sign is, look it up below and read how it works with your Aquarian Sun to blend your mind, soul and spirit.

♈ **With the Moon in ARIES, Sun in Aquarius,** you are likely to be ★ Observant, astute, self-interested, alert, emotionally detached, enthusiastic, independent, honest, devoted to truth, loyal, adventurous, hot-tempered, independent, courageous, prophetic, overly assertive, temperamental, insensitive, ambitious, self-reliant, energetic, emotionally bold and reckless, restless, speak before thinking, a fast communicator, soundly intellectual, acid-tongued, respectful of others' opinions, pioneering, original, forward-looking, lively, witty, frank, bright, off-the-wall, rebellious, an intelligent individualist, one who has moral integrity, and a maverick truth-seeker.

Sun/Moon Harmony Rating ★ 8 out of 10

♉ With the Moon in TAURUS, Sun in Aquarius, you are likely to be ★ Calm, level-headed, pragmatically intellectual, easy going, possessive, stubborn, materialistic, gentle, infinitely patient, slow and steady-paced, conflicted between security and freedom, tenacious, emotionally placid, devoted to causes, reluctant to listen to others' views if convinced your own are correct, logical and detached in emotional matters, stoic, faithful, friendly, capable, determined, resourceful, dependable, an eccentric entrepreneur, ambitious, peace-loving but strong-willed, reliable, philanthropic, thoughtful, realistic, sensible, persistent, and dedicated to grounding your inspiration and idealism.

Sun/Moon Harmony Rating ★ *5 out of 10*

♊ With the Moon in GEMINI, Sun in Aquarius, you are likely to be ★ A free spirit, changeable, friendly, bright, breezy, emotionally versatile, quick-witted, philosophical but flippant, perceptive, clever, inspiring, stimulating, sociable, detached, flexible yet stubborn, iconoclastic, curious, emotionally impulsive, restless, easily bored, logical, creative, progressive, communicative, strongly socially aware, unsentimental, emotionally naïve, gifted, a wonderful friend, original, popular, funny, easily swept away by ideas and concepts, open towards and perceptive of new ideas, idealistic, intellectual, squandering of your natural talents, reluctant to face the darker aspects of life, too busy to deal with feelings, and ruled by your mind rather than your gut instincts. **

Sun/Moon Harmony Rating ★ *9 out of 10*

♋ **With the Moon in CANCER, Sun in Aquarius,** you are likely to be ★ Passive, sensitive, intuitive, emotionally expressive, strongly socially conscious, compassionate, a kind-hearted rebel, sympathetic, shy, emotionally reticent, hidden, private, eccentric, peaceful, imaginative, poetic, intelligently kind, devoted to truth and the triumph of the human spirit, helpful, companionable, emotionally lofty, progressive but old-fashioned values, able to express Universal insights through personal projection, a sensitive individualist, self-protective, unconsciously prejudiced, likely to become absorbed with abstract causes which cuts you off from your feelings, and occasionally moved to emotional outbursts.

Sun/Moon Harmony Rating ★ *5 out of 10*

♌ **With the Moon in LEO, Sun in Aquarius,** you are likely to be ★ Proud, independent, individualistic, gentle on the surface with a great strength within, dramatic, a fearless defender of principles and causes, artistic, wise and generous in helping others, visionary, passionate, radiantly humanitarian, enthusiastic for new and original ideas, trustworthy, a good leader of groups, romantically imaginative, open, charismatic, powerful, extroverted, honest, passionate, warm, bold, inclined to get carried away by romance and idealism and forget to return to Earth, direct, vain, glamorising of others and failing to see their true colours, friendly, stubbornly controlling, generous, expressive, ambitious, despotic, self-centred, self-reliant, creative, emotionally radiating warmth, emotionally idealistic, luxury-loving, helpful, demonstrative, and creatively imaginative.

Sun/Moon Harmony Rating ★ *7 out of 10*

♍ **With the Moon in VIRGO, Sun in Aquarius,** you are likely to be ★ Puritanical, intelligent, judgemental, cool, calm and collected, aloof, critical, clever, discriminating, an emotional perfectionist, methodical, studious, a devoted researcher, helpful, a truth-seeker, serious, kind-hearted, innovative, mentally alert, unassuming, mentally dextrous, efficient, undemonstrative, caring, rigid, reserved, rebellious yet conventional, objectively rational, cool-headed, willing to help and do what needs to be done, altruistic, genuinely kind, bright, devoted to ideals, dry-witted, and radical yet uptight.

Sun/Moon Harmony Rating ★ *6 out of 10*

♎ **With the Moon in LIBRA, Sun in Aquarius,** you are likely to be ★ Lively, intellectual, able to work with principles easily, see life from endlessly new vantage points, sociable, refined, paradoxical, generally well-balanced and moderate, easy going, sporadically affectionate, popular, a hider of feelings, graceful, charming, approachable, tolerant, distanced from your true emotional power, accessible, civilised, sharing, gracious, cooperative, approval-seeking, hospitable, hedonistic, indecisive, interested in people, places and purposes globally, romantically idealistic, endearing, acutely observant, loving of people, quick witted, honest, shocking and delightful at the same time, colourfully persuasive, artistically sensitive, abstract, emotionally naïve, and conflicted between independence and needing others. **

Sun/Moon Harmony Rating ★ *9 out of 10*

♏ **With the Moon in SCORPIO, Sun in Aquarius,** you are likely to be ★ Intense, powerfully intellectual, forceful, highly charged, extreme and radical, possessive, keenly insightful, investigative, unbending, strong-willed, self-judging, a reformer, dominating, intensely dedicated to ideals, passionate, unyielding, resourceful, resilient, controlling, stubborn, persevering and thorough, devoted to truth at any cost, fiercely principled, psychologically penetrative, secretive, passionate yet dispassionate, loyal, emotional, courageously dedicated to reform and improvement for the welfare of others, an astute observer, perceptive, self-reliant, dogmatic, stern, exacting, potentially ruthless and manipulative, and emotionally powerful.

Sun/Moon Harmony Rating ★ *6 out of 10*

♐ **With the Moon in SAGITTARIUS, Sun in Aquarius,** you are likely to be ★ Eager, friendly, independent, idealistic, a traveller of body and mind, big-hearted, honest, adventurous, rationalising, impatient with petty details and restrictions of daily life, prone to preach when advancing causes, unaware of the subtleties of social intercourse, intellectual, inquisitive, an adventurer, able to see the 'big picture', distant from your feelings, emotionally reckless, a free spirit, non-committal, a good teacher, in possession of a zany sense of humour, far-sighted, intellectually speedy, optimistic, a lover of learning, inspiring, outrageous, aspiring, gregarious, socially concerned, broad-minded, rebellious, expansive, verbose, emotionally philosophical, freedom-seeking, and guided by reason rather than emotion.

Sun/Moon Harmony Rating ★ *9 out of 10*

♑ **With the Moon in CAPRICORN, Sun in Aquarius,** you are likely to be ★ Dependable, steadfast, resourceful, committed to causes, independent, driven to succeed, ambitious to make the world a better place, critical, reserved, withdrawn, cool, unemotional, wise, shrewd, organised, down-to-Earth, efficient, reliable, serious, sensible, materialistic, introverted, understanding of practical applications and wisdom, economical, brotherly, a practical reformer, 'a rebel with a cause', inventive, personally honourable, overly-strict when adhering to principles, fearless, uptight, socially rigid, self-contained, aware of human character, sardonically humorous, and willing to work in the present for the future good.

Sun/Moon Harmony Rating ★ *6.5 out of 10*

♒ **With the Moon in AQUARIUS, Sun in Aquarius,** you are likely to be ★ Friendly and tolerant, independent, idealistic, emotionally detached, eccentric, 'different', unconventional, aloof, paradoxical, imaginative, sympathetic, honest, original, forward-moving, inventive, impersonal in relationships, clear-headed, highly observant, acutely aware of the human condition, progressive, scientifically oriented, objective, living an unusual lifestyle in some way, well-meaning, open to the unusual, emotionally naïve, over-identifying with causes, blunt and insensitive when comparing people with your ideals, freedom-loving, unorthodox, impractical, loyal, humanitarian, globally aware, courageous and committed to your ideals, a law unto yourself, and in possession of an eternal sense of hope and belief in human potential.

Sun/Moon Harmony Rating ★ *8 out of 10*

♓ **With the Moon in PISCES, Sun in Aquarius,** you are likely to be ★ Highly imaginative, intuitive, with the ability to blend common sense and mysticism, over-idealistic, a chaser of spiritual rainbows, heart in the right place, good-natured, intriguing, kindly, friendly, emotionally intelligent, apt to wander off on your own and go into flights of fancy, hot and cold emotions, sentimental, gentle, accepting, understanding, independent but vulnerable, a thinker and a poet, altruistic, in possession of a Universal outlook, humorous, psychologically insightful, generous, receptive, creative, reverent, forgiving, devoutly committed to social causes, mysterious, empathetic, humanitarian, prone to drifting and wasting time in daydreams, impressionable, idealistic but easily swayed, gullible, impractical, evasive, sensitive, psychic, perceptive, able to mix and work with all types of people, and aware of the needs of others.

Sun/Moon Harmony Rating ★ *8 out of 10*

** If your Moon is in Gemini or Libra, your Sun and Moon will form what is known in astrology as a trine aspect. This aspect is the easiest, most flowing and harmonious astrological aspect, ensuring that your Sun and Moon, or spirit and soul, are well integrated. With both luminaries in Air signs, this gives them the best possible degree of complementary energy - a blending of the elements suggests a balanced expression of personality. One drawback of the trine aspect lies in the fact that its easy flow can be *too* harmonious; if our path is too smooth and difficulties don't arise to challenge us from time to time, we can often become lazy and complacent, stunting our growth and spiritual evolution. As Air signs, you share the art of sociability, are highly idealistic, affable, romantic, possess a good intellect, have a love of truth and beauty, are reasonable, broad-minded, independent but devoted to your ideals, have an artistic sensitivity, are tolerant, understanding, civilised and dignified, and have avant-garde tastes, but may be detached, cool, head over heart-oriented, and restless.

YOUR BODY & HEALTH

"A physician without a knowledge of astrology has no right to call himself a physician."
Hippocrates (born c. 460 BC)

Hippocrates, the fifth century BC Greek physician and 'father of medicine' and supposed author of the Hippocratic Oath, maintained that no one should be allowed to practise medicine who had not first studied astrology. Another Greek physician, Claudius Galen, brought together a huge range of knowledge and ideas in the second century AD which dominated medical practice until the 17th century. Among his teachings was a diagnostic technique which assumed that illnesses and their treatments were affected by and governed by the phases of the Moon. For centuries, astrology was a compulsory component of medical training (and still is in some natural medicine degrees), albeit only one aspect of diagnosis and treatment.

Medical or health astrology concerns particular ways of determining and interpreting an individual's horoscope with particular reference to health issues - diagnosis of current dis-eases, identification of areas of bodily weaknesses, and the prescription of natural cures and remedies. In ancient times, and still even today, the movement of the stars and planets was believed to affect bodily functions, and to cause ailments, or cure them.

During the Middle Ages, many drawings of the 'zodiac man' were made, which showed which signs of the zodiac were related to each part of the body, providing information as to the best times of the year to undertake cures for ailments affecting the corresponding body parts.

Health astrology persists today in many forms and among astrologers themselves, from whom clients seek counsel on health-related issues, and while it certainly cannot be used diagnose a condition or dis-ease, one's Sun sign, along with other factors of the natal chart, can definitely indicate potential problem areas of weakness or possible troubles. This branch of astrology has been found to be surprisingly accurate in most cases. While mostly accurate, none of the following information should ever be used as a substitute for professional medical advice should you be personally concerned about any of the conditions or afflictions listed for your Sun sign.

AQUARIAN HEALTH

Aquarius is associated with the Lower Legs (Calves, Ankles, Fibula, Tibia, Heels, Tendons, Anklebones), Blood Circulatory System, Heart Valves, Oxidation Processes of the Body, Pituitary Gland, Nerves, Sympathetic Nerve System, Motor Nerves, and Spinal Cord. Varicose veins, circulatory problems, nervous conditions, hypertension, weakness of limbs, ankle troubles, anaemia, cramps, blood pressure issues, anxiety, cold hands and feet, eye problems and haemorrhoids may be conditions which ail you.

Aquarius represents patterns of energy flow. Your nature is hot, moist and electric. Principal rulerships, some of which have already been mentioned previously, include the blood and circulation, nerve impulses and energy, lower leg, calves and ankles, mitochondria, the meridian system, auras and chakras, hypothalamus and the biorhythms. You respond well to alternative therapies and energetic forms of treatment.

Aquarians more than most, need an abundance of fresh air, sleep and regular exercise to stay healthy. You tend to eat unusual combinations of foods and large amounts of a single food, which can create health issues. You also need to take extra care with your usage of salt.

Aquarians are among the longest-lived types of the zodiac. Your constitution is wiry rather than strong and although you are quite willing to engage in physical toil if you have to, you're not really built for stamina or prolonged exertion.

You have tremendous reserves of nervous energy, and it is this rather than physical vitality that keeps you going at such a rate. When you have an idea or an ideal to work towards, you have the capacity for intense effort for lengthy periods - but your mental interest must be absorbed. You also need your friends around you; companionship is like a therapy to you whenever you feel jaded or depleted, and if you are denied this connection with a wide variety of people, you are likely to start to feel under par. Yet you also require very definite periods of seclusion, to relax in solitude or wander off alone into a forest to restore your mind, body and spirit. Your dynamism and volatile energies will quickly replenish if you do take this necessary time out when you need it. Often your manic mental activity can manifest as nervous complaints and stress-related conditions, which usually sort themselves out without much fuss, but the Water Bearer may develop phobias.

Aquarius seems to suffer according to the weather conditions - which are always too hot, too cold, too humid, or too dry. Circulatory problems and diseases of the blood and nervous system are common in Aquarians, and they are prone to varicose veins, and calf and ankle accidents or afflictions. There is also a connection with the heart through your opposite sign Leo, making you prone in later life to suffering from hardening of the arteries. This isn't usually a problem for too many Aquarians however, as you generally tend to live a moderate, temperate kind of lifestyle.

As Aquarius is linked with the sudden and unexpected energy of the planet Uranus, they may suffer from unpredictable, inexplicable illnesses that can then clear up again just as mysteriously. Uranus governs the Overall Brain, Cerebral and Nervous Functions, Rhythmic Systems, Spasms, Electricity, Nerves, Ankles, and the Circulation, these areas of your body may also need to be kept in check. Uranus is also associated with fractures, and if these occur, they usually strike below the knee. Uranus is also linked with the 'pineal body', the mysterious 'third eye', and believed to rule those parts of the eye which, when developed, can see the human aura. Furthermore, it has a marked influence over the nervous system, especially over the electrical impulses which pass between the nerve cells. With all this in mind, Aquarians often suffer from associated ailments, such as spasms, epilepsy, ruptures, accidents, strictures, cramps, malnutrition, breaks and circulatory disorders.

Keeping yourself in excellent health overall, with a special awareness of Aquarius' vulnerable points, is key to achieving all you set out to do, and getting the most out of your life!

THE CELL SALTS ★ ASTROLOGICAL TONICS

Homeopathy and astrology have colluded to provide a wonderful list of astrological tonics, one particularly suited to each of the twelve signs. These are called 'homeopathic cell salts', 'tissue salts' or 'biochemic cell salts', and are available in most health food stores, are inexpensive and easy to take. They are considered to be gentle, effective and safe, even for children, people in fragile health states, and the elderly. Although the full picture, drawn from a full natal horoscope, gives a fuller, more accurate idea of an individual's unique constitution, even simply working with one's date of birth can be enough for the medical astrologer to suggest the use of a cell salt based upon the correlation with an individual's Sun sign. As well as the cell salts having a significant effect upon physical ailments, they can also profoundly influence the subtle energy bodies, including the mental, emotional, etheric and spiritual. Although the most common use of these salts is based upon each salt's correspondence with a Sun sign, use of the cell salt related to one's Moon sign can assist with addressing deeper underlying emotional issues, such as anxiety, depression, panic and fear. Use of the cell salt relating to your Moon sign will therefore help to restore your sense of safety, balance, security and emotional resilience. In the first seven years of life, when the Moon is the most influential sphere in our lives, Lunar cell salts are the most appropriate choice as a remedy or tonic.

For specific health problems, take both the salt of your Sun or Moon sign, *and* the salt that pertains to the specific condition. The same principle applies to the Ascendant sign, as the First House represents one's physical health, and especially if the Sun or Moon is a rising planet, which means rulership of the whole chart. For the purposes of this book, however, the cell salt that correlates with your Sun sign only is outlined.

TISSUE SALT FOR AQUARIUS ★ NAT MUR.

Natrum muriaticum, or Nat Mur. (Sodium chloride) is the cell salt for Aquarius. Nat Mur. is simply salt, a substance present in the natural world in greater quantities than any other except water. It is essential to life and health. Any condition involving too much dryness or too much moisture indicates the use of this salt. Nat mur. has the effect of regulating fluids by attracting or drawing away water from affected parts of the body, to redistribute it wherever it is needed. Aquarius rules the circulation and blood, the ankles, the spinal cord and the electrical impulses of the nerves, and Nat mur. may help in supporting the smooth and even flow of electricity through and across the nerves. Symptoms of insufficient Nat mur. are insomnia, improper or dysfunctional nerve synapse firing, intermittent nerve pains, dry skin conditions, eczema, digestive complaints, dryness or excessive salivation in the mouth, watery colds, constipation or herpes and/or blisters on or around the mucus membranes. Nat mur. is otherwise known as sodium chloride, or table salt, and overall it is said to be good at regulating the water supply throughout the body, therefore affecting elimination and how cold or hot we feel regardless of the temperature.

AIR SIGN AQUARIUS & THE SANGUINE HUMOR

Greek physician Hippocrates (460 - 370 BC) theorised that certain human behaviours were caused by body fluids, called 'humours'. Later, Galen of Pergamon (AD 131 - 200), a Greek physician, developed the first typology of temperaments to encompass many facets of the human psyche and physiology. These also related to the classical elements of Fire, Earth, Air and Water - as choleric, melancholic, sanguine and phlegmatic respectively. According to the Greeks who developed the temperament theory (the word stems from the Latin word *temperamentum*, meaning mixture), temperament is the 'mixture' of qualities that combine to form elements in physics and humours in medicine. The Greeks sought equilibrium in the four qualities of hot, cold, wet (moist), and dry, the elements of Earth, Air, Fire and Water, and the four humours of choler or yellow bile, melancholer or black bile, blood and phlegm. If balance was achieved, the person was said to be well- or even-tempered, and the importance of determining the temperament allowed for imbalances to be treated.

In ancient times, each of the four types of humours corresponded to a different personality type, which were associated with a domination of various biological functions. It was suggested that the temperaments came to clearest manifestation in childhood, between around the ages of six and fourteen of age, after which they become subordinate, but still influential, factors in our personality. It is important to note that your temperament is not your personality. However, your personality can incorporate parts of the temperament in its expression. Personality is shaped by both external and internal factors, whereas the temperament is innate, an inborn, inherent part of each individual.

The Air element corresponds with the humour sanguine, which is characterised by quick, impulsive and relatively short-lived reactions. Sanguine types are analogous with Air, which is the main element in spring, the season with which this temperament has an affinity. Sanguine characters are ruled by Venus and Jupiter, hence the labels Venusian and Jupiterian Sanguines.

Sanguine types are driven by the need for attention and acceptance, social contact, relating, relationships, and trying to impress others. A sanguine disposition represents positivity, optimism, extroversion, expressiveness, talkativeness, and light-heartedness. You are generally responsive, carefree, easy going and lively.

Overall, a sanguine disposition represents sociability and openness. Its taste is bitter, its nature acidic, its indication blood. The sanguine humour is associated with the *gas* ^ body, and with hot and moist conditions.

Additionally, the ethereal (or vital) body, comprises four ethers or subtle fluids, which are governed by the four Fixed signs of the zodiac: Taurus, Leo, Scorpio and Aquarius. Aquarius corresponds to the *mirror ether*, which stimulates and coordinates the thought functions of the physical brain, as well as controlling our desires and actions.

^ A couple of thousand years ago, the Mesopotamians, Chinese and Egyptians, and more recently the Arabs, practised a medicine called 'of three bodies'. According to the doctors of the ancient world (who often practised as astrologers as well), a human being had three bodies: the physical body, the ethereal (or vital) body and the astral body, imparting a holistic approach to health. In modern medicine, usually only the physical body is focused upon fully. According to tradition, this physical body comprises three principles or states corresponding to three primordial elements: *solid* (Earth), *liquid* (Water) and *gas* (Air). This is the material body, the physical outer cover of muscles, nerves and organs held together by the skeleton. The Fire element corresponds with the *astral* body, which sits outside the physical body in one's auric field.

MONEY ATTRIBUTES

Colour for Increased Earning Power ★ Aqua

The following plants can be used by all zodiac signs to assist in attracting money ★ Ginger, Allspice, Clover, Orange, Marjoram, Cinnamon, Sassafras, Woodruff, Bergamot, Tonka Beans, Heliotrope, Alfalfa, Coltsfoot, Thyme, Mace, Irish Moss, Clove, Almond, Corn, Honeysuckle, Sesame, Nutmeg, Vetiver, Poppy, Jasmine, Dill and Elder Flower. To attract luck and success, try using any of the above, combined with any of the following: Alfalfa Seeds, Basil, Mustard Seeds, Vervain Leaves, Poppy Seeds, Rosemary, Lemon, Anise and Holly.

Striving for financial gain and abundance with a healthy inner moral compass is, in my view, one of the most noble goals we can set for ourselves. When we have more money, we are better placed to help ourselves and of course others; after all, as Abraham Maslow's Hierarchy of Needs model (1943) attests, once our primary and base survival needs have been satisfied, we can then advance higher towards loftier achievements, such as self-confidence, creativity and self-actualisation. Prosperity allows us to turn our attention to these more transcendental matters - to reach for lives not just of material comfort and luxuries, but of meaning, generosity, balance, harmony, fulfilment and joy. Our Sun sign can offer clues as to how we go about acquiring, earning, saving, maintaining, and allowing the overall flow of giving and receiving money. What's *your* money style?

Aquarian writer W. Somerset Maugham once said, "Money is like a sixth sense without which you cannot make a complete use of the other five." He also quoted, "Money is the string with which a sardonic destiny directs the motions of its puppets." These statements reveal much about the Water Bearer's financial nature. It is a rare Aquarian who pursues money for its own sake. You may be shrewd, clever, successful and even have expensive tastes, but you are not avaricious. To you, money is indeed the sixth sense. You tend to take financial gain for granted, as it always seems to be there when you need it, and it flows naturally when you are doing the right thing, trusting your instincts and acting on hunches and inspired ideas.

Aquarians are either frugal or impulsive in their spending habits, depending on which planetary ruler is strongest. If Saturn is strong, you are tight-fisted and careful, knowing to the cent how much money you have. If Uranus is strong, your financial world is usually in chaos, fuelled by mounting debts and unusual business schemes. Aquarians are generally not spendthrifts however, caring more for ideals than for material possessions, and you are intelligent enough to discern what is a wise investment and what is not. Your innate futuristic thinking can make you have almost prophetic visions about your future financial standing, which you should tap into, to your advantage. Your instincts are usually excellent, scrupulous even, as are your potential money-making abilities - and both will work best when you're not even trying. Just like you don't make a conscious effort to be intuitive, money will similarly just arrive as a side-effect of trying to accomplish another aim altogether. Therefore, it would do you well to explore the possibility of doing professionally an aspect of what you are already doing voluntarily. Which brings me to the next point of the Aquarian financial nature: that of compassion and generosity, which comes naturally to you, but can sometimes get the better of you. Many Aquarians are charitable and philanthropic, due to their aim to achieve a better lot for all, but these laudable qualities can also place an enormous burden on your resources and monetary status.

Security is of less concern to the Water Bearer than freedom; and indeed, money buys you freedom and independence, which enable you to live the life you please. You may create money through inventions, your unique talents, or genius ideas that no one else has thought of. A brilliant invention or unique concept, borne out of your innate desire to improve mankind, could well make your fortune. Aquarians, more so than any other Sun sign, have fine talents and often have incipient genius lying latent and undeveloped in their subconscious, and unfortunately it may only be on rare occasions that these are ever called to the surface. Many Aquarians, apparently quite ordinary and undistinguished, might rise to a high place in the world if they would but apply themselves to developing these hidden powers. Self-confidence, overcoming your fixed obstinacy, recognition of worthwhile ideas, and the ability to share and generate those ideas, are needed to pull it off.

COLOURS

Chromatomancy, or divination by colour, is a form of energy therapy that has been used for thousands of years by many different cultures. It works on the principle that we make both instinctive and rational choices or preferences based on circumstances which are already present in ourselves; colour also has an effect on the energy in an environment, and we in turn respond consciously or subconsciously to our surroundings. If we look at the causes, and try to understand the reasons, as to why we are so receptive to one particular colour over another, we will see that there is a subtle link between certain hues and our emotional and instinctive individual reactions. The colour which we give to things results from a combination of three elements:

1. The light or the vibration of a body;

2. The context in which it is found and the interaction between its own light and that of its environment;

3. The sensitivity of the eye's retina which sees the body in question. Because of this, a colour can vary, depending on the individual's perceptions, namely, his sensitivity, his mood, and his view of reality. For a long time, people have understood that their vision of reality depends a lot on their moods, feelings and emotions.

Chromatotherapy, or colour healing, stems from this body of evidence, and its main application is the use of colours for healing purposes. Colours are generally associated with characteristics, feelings, stones, metals, plants and flowers, planets and even the zodiac signs. In varying cultures, they play a significant role in ceremonies and regalia.

We vibrate to the frequency of colour, shown through its continual movement and change in our aura ^. One of the most beautiful examples of colour is the rainbow. This architect of colour is caused by the refraction and internal reflection of light in raindrops. Colour can be perceived as either a pigment, or as illumination. The colour spectrum can be divided into eight main colours: red, orange, yellow, green, turquoise, blue, violet and magenta. Each colour has a wavelength and frequency that carry different therapeutic qualities which have indirect effects upon our health and bodily systems, and because of this, coupled with the fact that we as living energy centres emanate colour, colour can be a great medium in healing, calming, energising, increasing and attracting.

Aristotle, in the fourth century BCE, considered blue and yellow to be the true primary colours and related them to life's polarities: Sun and Moon, male and female, stimulation and sedation, in and out, expansion and contraction. He also associated colours with the four elements of Fire, Earth, Air and Water. Hippocrates, the father of medicine, used colour extensively in medicinal healing and recognised that the therapeutic effects of a white violet differed from those of a purple one. In the fifteenth century, Paracelsus placed particular importance on the role of colour in healing.

Each Sun sign and planetary body has a specific colour or colours which when used in combination with wishing rituals, can enhance their power immensely. Coloured candles can be used to good effect, as the fire energy of the flame/s increases the power of any wish, and flames are also a useful aid to meditating on, focusing upon or clarifying what you want. Coloured candles help to focus the energy for whatever purpose the colour is in sympathy with (e.g. green for money, pink for romance, orange for joy, etc.)

With all this in mind, wearing or using your Sun sign or ruling planet's magical colour/s on a regular basis will undoubtedly bring great benefits.

^ The aura is defined as an energy field, which interpenetrates with, and radiates beyond, the physical body. Clairvoyantly seen, the aura is full of light, colour and shade. The trained healer or seer sees or senses indications within the aura as to the spiritual, physical and emotional state of the individual. Much of the auric colour and energy emanates from the chakras.

YOUR LUCKY COLOURS

For Aquarius ★ Electric Blue, Ultramarine Blue, Turquoise, Sky Blue, Electric Green, Violet, Purple, Grey, Deep Amethyst

For Uranus ★ Light blue, Silvery White, Cobalt Blue, Shocking Pink *, electric and glaring hues, fluorescent colours, and stripes and swirls of many colours

* A trend-setting pink, which was an attention-grabbing magenta, was named 'shocking pink' in the thirties, 'hot pink' in the fifties, and 'kinky pink' in the sixties, was a fashion leader and bold statement in each of these eras. The colour pink came into vogue through its proliferated use in the cosmetics industry during the sixties - a most defining and memorable decade - when no stylish woman would leave the house without her trusty pink lipstick. At other times, it took back position in the closet and was dismissed as vulgar, sensational, ostentatious and showy.

Your zany style is usually years ahead of everyone else, and you reflect this by wearing bold colours which usually make an impact, are eye-catching or add shock value: such as electric blue, turquoise and aquamarine.

Each of the eight colours of the rainbow spectrum also has a complementary colour to which it is matched. Red is complementary to turquoise, orange to blue, yellow to violet, and green to magenta. If these colour pairs enhance each other's most spellbinding qualities and energies, perhaps you could try wearing your Sun sign's lucky colour with its matching complementary colour in order to produce extra magical results! Your lucky Aquarian colours are turquoise, which complements red, electric blue and purple. Now you know your colours, you can dress for success!

FEATURE COLOURS ★ TURQUOISE, ELECTRIC BLUE & PURPLE

★ TURQUOISE ★

Planetary Association ★ Jupiter

Healing Qualities ★ Refreshing, cleansing, calming but invigorating, uplifting, creative, open communication, clarity of thought, inner healing through empathy

Complementary Colour ★ Red or Orange

Turquoise is a colour of Jupiter and can represent Air and the sky. It is a variation of the colour blue, and is derived by mixing together blue and green. It can veer towards either of these colours but is best known as possessing a vibrant, opaque bright bluish tone. This vivid colour, reminiscent of a tropical ocean, is both invigorating and calming. It promotes emotional balance and stability, recharging our spirits during times of mental stress and fatigue. As the spiritual stone of the Native Americans and the Aztecs, turquoise symbolises truth and aids communication on all levels. It indicates a dynamic quality of being, a highly energised personality, positive influence over others, and the ability to project oneself to beneficial effect - great for getting those brilliant ideas across! Good for heightening creativity and sensitivity, it helps to sharpen our powers of observation and perception. Turquoise is a wonderful all-round healer and general tonic for the immune system. It is ultimately the colour of calm, serenity and spiritual harmony.

★ ELECTRIC BLUE ★

Complementary Colour ★ Red or Orange

A steely, brilliant light blue, electric blue has a vivid magnificence that is awe-inspiring and pleasing to the eye. It is a wondrous version of the colour blue, and can also resemble the shade of turquoise, in a heightened, more luminous form. The colour blue symbolises inspiration, devotion, truth, higher wisdom, peace and tranquillity. It is calming and is an excellent healing colour. Blue also creates a sense of space, so any room or area painted in this colour will appear larger. Because of its calming vibes, it is a soothing and useful colour with which to treat headaches, tension, stress and insomnia.

PURPLE

"When I am an old woman I shall wear purple."
Jenny Joseph

Planetary Associations ★ Uranus, Jupiter, the Moon

Healing Qualities ★ Powerful, Psychic, Beautiful, Awareness, Inspiring, High Ideals, Wisdom, Protective, Spiritual Awareness, Creativity

Keywords ★ Problem-solving, Intuitive, Psychic Realm, Resurrection, Royalty (red + blue), Spiritual Power, Dignity, Piety, Creativity, Uranus, the Moon, Truth, the Cosmos

The colour of Uranus and of the element of ether or spirit, purple may also be used to represent the Moon's power in healings. It is the last visible colour before ultraviolet, so it is often associated with time, space and the Universe itself. Purple is an intriguing colour because it combines and balances the diametrically opposed attributes of two colours: the fire and passion of red, and the coolness and calm of blue. This quality makes purple both an exciting and thought-provoking colour that elicits mixed reactions, able to imply either greater wisdom or underlying confusion. Despite this conflict, it has been said that more than three quarters of children prefer this shade to any other. It can enhance ambition, astral work, compassion, psychic abilities, spirituality, and improve luck and spiritual love. A colour of transformation at a deep level, purple denotes spiritual peace and awareness. Purple crystals such as amethyst and purple jade, are associated with realisation and illumination, and as such are perfect stones for those wishing to succeed; they can be used to attract good fortune into your life. Lighter shades of purple, such as lilac and lavender, evoke gentle feelings of romance, comfort and nostalgia, and the warmth of pale purple is less striking than that of other bright shades such as pink and orange, because it is tempered with the coolness of blue. Striking a balance between the two, purple can therefore be soft and atmospheric, suggesting distance and aloofness, or whimsical and full of fancy, the colour of first love and of devotion. The blue and red elements within purple also symbolise powerful fusion of the celestial and the Earthly. Pale purples are connected to spiritual enlightenment, to the Third Eye and to contacting the spirit world.

You can use purples to provide protective energy and enhance your strength and psychic abilities. It is associated with the Crown chakra, the link between yourself and Nirvana, or complete enlightenment and, when balanced, will render you happy, contented and fulfilled. Purple in Feng Shui is associated with the Fire element and is linked with the south and with determination, joy and inner fire. As the colour of the south, it is connected with the desire for fame, status and recognition. Purple is the colour of mystery and nobility, merging the tranquillity of blue with the heat and boldness of red. Because it combines the energy and vitality of red with the stability of blue, it is the perfect colour to stimulate the mind while keeping stress at bay. A very spiritual and relaxing colour, its connections with opulence, nobility, dignity, power and wealth stretch back to ancient times, when it was believed to have been Cleopatra's favourite colour; an in Ancient Rome, a crimson substance was first extracted from molluscs and then used to create a purple dye that coloured the ornate garments of the emperors. Shades of purple have been shown to help calm people with nervous or mental imbalances. It can stimulate your imagination or inspire you and can improve your creativity. People who are drawn to this colour often have an interest in spiritual growth. During the sixties, the colour purple was considered unconventional and rebellious, and came to symbolise the decade's search for freedom and a more Universal love. Overall, purple is a common colour in magic; a purple candle represents Uranus, Jupiter and the power of the Moon; it can be used to enhance luck or telepathy, while a purple 'spell' bag can be used for protection and healing. The herb and colour lavender is also an essential ingredient in any ritual or magical work, being used to make wishes, attract your soul mate or for healing spells. Purple magic is, in essence, potent.

Blue (particularly in shades of turquoise and electric blue), and its complementary rainbow spectrum colour red, as well as purple, are Aquarius's special LUCKY colours! These can be worn or otherwise used together to dazzling and mesmerising effect.

AQUARIUS' CHAKRA CORRESPONDENCE
★ CROWN

The word 'chakra' comes from the Sanskrit and means 'wheel', disc' or 'circle'. Chakras are vitally important to your physical health, emotional wellbeing and spiritual growth, and are regarded as a complete integrated system that works holistically. The chakras are funnel-shaped spinning energy vortexes of multi-coloured light. These swirling vortexes of energy absorb and distribute life-force, the subtle energy known as *prana*. The seven master chakras - Root, Sacral, Solar Plexus, Heart, Throat, Third Eye and Crown - lie in the centre line of the body, with the first five embedded within the spinal column. Each chakra vibrates at a different vibrational frequency and on a different note, and responds to specific life issues or 'thought forms'.

The lower body chakras deal with physical issues. As we move up the body, the chakras correspond to increasingly spiritual concerns. As a consequence, each chakra's energy vibrates at a different rate, depending on whether they govern earthbound or ethereal issues. The lower chakras have slower and denser vibrations, while the higher chakras spin at faster speeds with higher vibrations.

Because the chakras have no physical manifestation and cannot be located using any scientific instrument, they have tended to be viewed with scepticism by many Western medical professionals, a distinction they share with energy points in acupuncture and the notion of meridians. Instead, they are believed to have been sensed intuitively by many people over many centuries, and indeed people in yoga positions and in deep meditation have reported experiencing the sensation of a surge of energy rising from the base of the spine and emerging through the top of the head. Some people have even said they have seen points of blue light when their *kundalini* energy has risen from the lowest chakra to the highest, as well as experiencing a profound sense of happiness and ecstasy.

In summary, the Universal Life Force enters the body through the Crown chakra at the top of the head. As it works its way through the body, it flows through the other centres. As it spreads to the Base chakra, it is said to arouse the kundalini energy, which yogis believe sleeps in a coiled serpentine form.

The chakra associated with Aquarius is the seventh, or Crown chakra, which governs spiritual wisdom, higher communication and enlightenment. This is the highest chakra of the seven master chakras, and is a receptacle for guidance and understanding from higher 'planes', letting in Universal and Divine knowledge.

CROWN CHAKRA

Location ★ Top of Head
Colour ★ Purple, Violet
Concerned with ★ Spiritual Wisdom & Enlightenment
Gland ★ Pituitary
Essential Oils ★ Neroli, Elemi, Violet Wood, Cedarwood, Frankincense, Linden Blossom, Jasmine, Rose, Rosewood
Animals ★ No Animals
Shape ★ Upward Triangle
Element ★ Consciousness/Knowing/Cosmic
Planets ★ Uranus
Zodiac Signs ★ Aquarius
Flower ★ 1,000-petalled Lotus
Energy State ★ Information

Positive Expression ★ Spiritual, At Oneness, Connectedness, Divine Love

Negative Expression (Blockage)★ Self-Righteous, spacey, ungrounded, impractical, alienated, indecisive, lack of common sense, difficulty with finishing things, depressed, confused, plagued by a sense of meaninglessness, delusional

The Crown chakra is located just above the crown of the head and does not, therefore have a 'physical' position. Its Sanskrit name is *sahasrara*, and its symbol is the thousand-petal white lotus flower. This is the level of super-consciousness or *samadhi*, a plane beyond time, space and consciousness. Balance in this chakra is expressed as cosmic connection and consciousness. It corresponds to the pineal gland and the cerebral cortex nerve plexus. Crystals that can be used to cleanse and balance this chakra are clear or violet stones, including: Amethyst, Clear Quartz, Diamond, Angelite, Danburite, Ametrine, Charoite Azeztulite, Lepidolite, Phenacite, Selenite, Tanzanite and Sugilite.

LUCKY CAREER TIPS & PATHS THAT WILL MAKE YOUR BANK BALANCE & SPIRITUAL SELF SOAR

The branch of astrology known as 'vocational astrology' encompasses the areas of one's calling, career path, or ideal profession. Careers, jobs, professions and occupations can all mean different things to different people, but to simplify the definition, I refer to a vocation as one's true calling, one's authentic path, and a dynamic way of life which pays an income in some form and leads to a deep fulfilment of personal and spiritual needs. An ideal vocation will provide self-fulfilment, ego satisfaction, and feed one's inner drive to achieve what they ultimately wish to achieve, whether that be to gain recognition, wealth or approval, to travel, to learn and fulfil an inner need for knowledge, an urge to serve others in some way, or an urge to improve personal, societal or Universal conditions.

In order to gain ultimate fulfilment and self-esteem, we all need a purpose in life. Many people gain this through their work, providing the job or career they choose suits their temperament, talents and aspirations. If our professional life is unsatisfactory or disharmonious in any way, frustration, unhappiness and even despair can result. Although your whole horoscope would need to be drawn up and interpreted in order to gain more substantial, deeper insights into your ideal career and purpose, you can begin by being guided by your Sun sign, which can give you many pointers to a suitable, and therefore successful, career path. You just never know, something in the following might jump out at you and make your soul dance immediately - and hopefully all the way to the bank!

With your Sun in Aquarius, you are inventive, original and have a systematic way of thinking. Computers, modern technology, and anything new or cutting edge and mentally challenging will attract you. Being a humanitarian and revolutionary at heart, alternative healing paths (especially within groups or communities) and social groups and issues will also appeal, for you love to effect societal change. In no way could you be described as conventional, so it is natural that many Aquarians choose a career which is different, unorthodox, unexpected, or embraces the unusual or alternative. This is the sign of inventors, scientists, social workers, brilliant thinkers, humanists, occultists, political reformers and revolutionaries. Alternative therapies, gadgets, coming up with new and innovative ideas, or working for political reform, are all hobbies which often develop into careers. Your ideal vocation allows you freedom, independence, autonomy, occasionally working within groups and to invent new systems which benefit society.

For the more Saturnian or conventional Aquarians, the following fields may hold appeal: Aviation, Counselling, Electrics and Electronics, Radar, Sonar or Television, Photography, Research, Selling Unusual Antiques or Books, Specialist Hobbies or Social Clubs.

Ideal careers for Aquarius overall are: Scientist, Astrologer, Inventor, Radiologist, Art Dealer, Television Broadcaster, Ecologist, Human Rights Officer, Protestor, Radical Healer, Magician, Laser Technician, Recording Studio Engineer, Telecommunications Worker, Social Worker, New Age Healer, Aid Worker, Politician, Laboratory Technician, Sociologist, Aeronautic Worker, Aviator, Broadcaster, Faith Healer, New Age Teacher, Nuclear Physicist, Science and Space Technologist, Alternative Health Worker or Self-Development Guru. Many of these professions reflect the fact that Aquarians are ahead of their time.

The Aquarian mind is scientific and inventive with finely balanced powers of reasoning. Being also kind, tolerant and diplomatic in your view of life, you would do well to share your ideas and ideals through writing, journalism, research and even acting, as you also possess an accessible imaginative quality.

Of course this does not account for everyone born under the sign of the Water Bearer, but for those of you who are strongly in tune with your ruling planet Uranus, there is certainly an element of the 'avant garde' in your nature and you don't fit the standard, conventional mould. Essentially, Uranus rules astrologers, anything to do with electricity, natural and social scientists, aviators, inventors, numerologists, and those delving into the occult sciences in general. Its influence is most pronounced in all aspects of computer programming and technology, space science, and concepts in futuristic and/or technological advancement. Some purely Uranian types will be fiercely self-sufficient and radical nonconformists who prefer to blaze new trails, challenge the status quo, alter the world for the better, and experiment with new progressive ideas or methods, carving for themselves a deeply life-changing and original career as they go - and might even reinvent themselves into eccentric millionaires in the meantime!

LUCKY PLACES WHERE YOUR ENERGY IS HEIGHTENED

As the Air element and Sanguine humour corresponds with hot and moist conditions, warm, humid, tropical places suit your constitution, disposition and temperament. The following nations, countries and cities are also places whose vibrations are closely allied with the sign of Aquarius: Australia, Chile, St Vincent and the Grenadines, Venezuela, Finland, Sri Lanka, Ethiopia, Italy (Trent), The Vatican City, Prussia, Lithuania, Japan, Jordan, Canada, Germany (Bremen, Hamburg), Liechtenstein, Sweden (Stockholm), Austria (Salzburg), Russia (Leningrad, St Petersburg, Moscow, Siberia), Cyprus and Scandinavia. Israel, Nepal, Gambia, Great Britain, Iran, Abyssinia, New Zealand, North America (Los Angeles) and some parts of Arabia and Poland, are also in tune with the Aquarian energy, as are hippie trails, communes, and offbeat and unusual places. A group adventure to the ski slopes or a palm-tree fringed tropical island paradise upon which a hippie retreat or commune exists, and places which boast quirky architecture and futuristic designs, could very well be your ticket to Aquarian heaven!

GEMS & CRYSTALS

"People love stones, and apparently stones love people. Like the angels they may be, they seem endlessly willing to serve the wellbeing of humans and to help us achieve our desires …Unlike people of the ancient past, we now have access to virtually the entire mineral kingdom. We have the opportunity to work like modern alchemists, combining and arranging the stones and their currents, looking for combinations and patterns that can help us enhance our inner and outer lives."
Robert Simmons, *Stones of the New Consciousness*

Each crystal and mineral of the Earth embodies different qualities, patterns or potential expressions of the Divine language, the silent whispers of the Universe. If we can accept the fact that the human body is a sophisticated, multi-faceted antenna system comprised of a crystalline matrix that is constantly transmitting and receiving all manner of energies, it could then be assumed that energy and body workers who use quartz, shells and stones, which are also crystalline materials, have the power to promote resonant interactions with the liquid 'crystal' structures found in human tissues. It could even be said that we are all made of essentially the same substances and structures, and that crystals and gemstones vibrate at varying energetic levels which can connect with our own in order to 'buzz' and dance together to make a harmonious Uni-verse both within and without.

All crystals work through vibrational balancing and by channelling energy. The magic of crystals is in their colour, which is determined by the rate at which their atoms vibrate; these vibrations can be matched to the energy given by your own body's aura. And just as light can be focused and refracted through gemstones, so too can all kinds of psychic energy, from healing energies to Divine communications.

Gemstones can help us attune to higher vibrations and bring them into our own experience and being. This theory of crystal resonance suggests that the characteristic energy patterns emanated by any stone can be transferred into the 'liquid crystal medium' of our bodies through resonance. Our bodies, being composed of these tuneable liquids, can mimic and mirror any consistent vibrational pattern with which we come into contact; we can therefore resonate with the healthful qualities of various crystals and minerals.

Crystals and precious stones have been valued throughout world cultures over many centuries for their healing virtues and capacities to imbue courage, strength, invulnerability, clairvoyance, love and numerous other qualities. Wearing gemstones is one of the simplest and most effective self-healing practices you can undertake, and wearing or carrying those stones whose vibrations correspond with the qualities you wish to embody brings their energetic currents into engagement with your body.

Over time the phenomenon of energetic integration, may be felt tangibly and your own vibrational field may internalise the stone's currents and adjust to them and effectively 'store' them, making them, eventually, a part of your own vibrational make-up. And we seem to know from the resonances we feel within our bodies when in contact with these gemstones, that crystals emanate tangible, if oft immeasurable, currents.

Crystals act as transmitters and amplifiers of your will or intentions - as long as your will or intentions are in sympathy with the crystal's energy. The mineral kingdom refers to stones, minerals and crystals and the associations and vibrations they carry. When working with stones, we are working with several different layers of spiritual energies, and although they can be regarded as inanimate 'psychic batteries', they are actually moving, vibrating masses of energy which transmit potential and power into our lives. Some crystals and stones even have receptive powers, which means they can absorb energy and retain it within until cleansed or re-programmed.

Although it is untrue that the only stones you can usefully wear are the ones astrologically matched with your Sun sign or ruling planet, those which align with your Sun sign or ruling planet are your most fortuitous and therefore strongest 'attractors' and 'amplifiers'.

Twelve oracular gemstones were described in the Bible, as the author of *Exodus* (28-15 and 17-21) knew them. Yahweh spoke to Moses about the breastplate he would have to wear to train for priesthood, and described it to him in these words: "And thou shalt make the breastplate of judgement with cunning work; ... And thou shalt set in it settings of stones, even four rows of stones; the first row shall be a sardius, a topaz, and a carbuncle. And the second row shall be an emerald, a sapphire and a diamond. And the third row an opal, an agate and an amethyst. And the fourth row a beryl, and an onyx, and a jasper; they shall be set in hold in their inclosings. And the stones shall be with the children ... (all) twelve (of them)." Given that the compilers of the Bible lived during a time when astrological belief was prevalent in Babylon, it seems valid to assert that these previously named gemstones would have some astrological basis. Further, since these ancient people supposedly made correlations between each of the twelve precious stones, and one of the twelve zodiac signs, there are seven crystalline systems set down in crystallography (or the science of the laws which influence the formation, structure and geometric, physical and chemical properties of crystallised matter) as analogous with the seven traditional ruling planets of the zodiac.

However, nobody is under the rule of one planet alone. We are all in essence a complex mixture of every planet, many elements and varying aspects, depending on their positions, placements and prominence in our birth chart. Everything that goes on in the skies above us affects what is going on here on Earth, and also *within* us. Your lucky stones are to assist you to tune into your Sun sign's energy and planetary influences, but you are by no means limited to the ones listed for your sign alone. Above all, let your stones, whichever ones you choose, work for you and allow them to transport your very own unique and magical energy into the wider Universe.

> "Beautiful and strong is the material of stones, but more beautiful and much more powerful is the mystery that emanates from them."
>
> **Chinese Poet & Alchemist, Li Po, 8th Century A.D.**

★ CLEAR QUARTZ ★

The Master Healer ★ *For All Zodiac Signs*

A common, well-known and popular gem, clear quartz (sometimes known as rock crystal) is an all-purpose 'jack-of-all-trades' stone. It amplifies the magic of any work you do or wishes you make. It is connected with all the chakras and increases the power of all other crystals. Clear quartz is a deep soul cleanser, which unblocks and regulates energy and emotions on all levels. It is balancing and harmonising. In various cultures, quartz crystal is reputed to be the most powerful crystal, the 'grandfather crystal', and the 'chief of the Stone People'. Clear quartz is also considered to be the only gemstone that is modifiable to suit your needs *, as other crystals automatically contain and retain their own specific resonance or natural signature. In essence, clear quartz is the most easily programmable and the most overall healing and readily accessible crystals of the mineral kingdom, holding a unique importance in the Universe of gems. And because of its all-encompassing nature and wide-ranging healing abilities, it has zodiacal affinities with all the signs.

* To program your clear quartz crystal, simply hold it on your Third Eye chakra (between and just above the

physical eyes) and concentrate on the purpose for which you wish to use it. Be positive and receptive while you allow your crystal to fill with this energy. If you wish, you could also state the intention of the programming out loud, for example, 'I program this crystal for love / healing / meditation / abundance / protection or (insert your own word here)'. You could also run your clear quartz crystal under running water, allow it to dry naturally, then hold the stone with both hands, bring it up to your mouth and blow into it sharply three times in order to impregnate it with your own breath. Then, hold it firmly in one hand and silently invite and welcome it into your life as a friend, helper and guide.

AQUARIAN & URANIAN LUCKY CRYSTALS, STONES & GEMS

Aquarius birth stones ★ Amethyst, Garnet, Aquamarine

January birth stones ★ Zircon, Garnet

February birth stones ★ Amethyst, Hyacinth

Amethyst, Garnet, Aquamarine (your three primary birthstones), Zircon (January birth stone), Hyacinth (February birth stone), Jacinth, Jargoon (Uranus), and Blue Sapphire (Saturn) are your luckiest gems, and one or more of these gems should be worn about your person to ensure good luck and increase your magnetism. Magnetite, Sugilite, Tourmaline, Dermantine, Apatite, Jade, Diamond, Bixbyite, Blue Obsidian, Lapis Lazuli, Chrysoprase, Blue Celestite, Azurite, Spirit Cactus Quartz, Fuchsite, Boji Stone,

Black Pearl, Slate, Hematite, Blue Quartz, Cavansite, Amber (Uranus), Angelite, Blue Lace Agate, Labradorite, Clear Quartz, Moonstone, Imperial Topaz, Fluorite, Antacamite, Tibetan Quartz, Titanium Quartz, Larimar and Turquoise also align with Aquarius's energy.

CRYSTALS & THE PLANETS

All the Vedic texts agree in relating gems to planets. This verse from the *Jatax Parijat* links each gem to a planet:

> *'The ruby is the gem of the Lord of the Day (the Sun),*
> *The shining pearl is the gem of the cold Moon,*
> *Red coral is the gem of Mars,*
> *The emerald is the gem of noble Mercury,*
> *Yellow sapphire is the gem of Jupiter, instructor of gods,*
> *Diamond is the gem of Venus, instructor of demons,*
> *Blue sapphire is the gem of Saturn.'*

Each planet influences its gem, and their curative power varies according to the position of its planet in the zodiac. Ayurvedic medicine has always paid attention to these details in their healing practices, often advising people to wear their corresponding zodiacal stone as a ring or a talisman.

CRYSTALS & THE ELEMENTS

Crystals are inextricably linked to the four elements, from their original creation to their potency and use in magical rituals and healing. Formed by the combination, in varying conditions, of different physical elements, such as metals, non-metals and gases, some stones require the enormous heat generated by volcanoes or deep thermal currents to bond their molecular makeup, while others may require pressure or water sources. The effects of the four elements of Fire, Earth, Air and Water is evident in these formation processes. The heat generated by Fire, pressure from the Earth, and the chemical reactions involved in absorbing elements from the Air and Water, all demonstrate the four elements in action to produce the correct conditions and ingredients necessary for the creation of crystals, lending them each their unique qualities.

CRYSTALS & THE AIR ELEMENT

The influence of the Air element may seem less apparent as its effects often occur invisibly, but its nature and essence are very important to some crystals. The most obvious manifestation of Air is in filling spaces; such as bubbles in crystals or the hollows in geodes. Air also provides the elements necessary for chemical reactions to occur during crystal formation. As the element of the intellect, knowledge, mind and clarity, symbolically Air can also fill you with ideas and enhance mental focus. Airy crystals can therefore assist in the formulation of concepts and plans, to focus your thoughts and to make decisions.

Some Airy crystals are ★ Sapphire, Kunzite, Chalcedony, Turquoise, Lapis Lazuli, Agate, Sodalite, Opal and Rose Quartz.

THE CRYSTALLINE SYSTEM OF YOUR TRADITIONAL RULING PLANET SATURN

Associated with your traditional ruling planet Saturn, are Black Coral, Carnelian, Jet, Onyx and Black Pearl. This is the second crystalline system, known as quadratic, that is having an upright prism with a square base, and its characteristics seem to be connected with this planet. The stone which perhaps represents this system best, the Wulfenite (only relatively recently discovered), is nothing other than lead molybdite, which is analogous with Saturn.

SATURN'S GEMSTONE ASSOCIATION

★ **Blue Sapphire** ★ The hardest crystal after diamond, sapphire has long held a reputation for its amazing spiritual as well as physical properties. Especially prized by the ancient Greeks and appearing throughout their mythology, those who wished to put a question to the famous Delphic Oracle had to wear a sapphire. There are many legends surrounding this luminous blue stone: The Ten Commandments were said to be written on tablets of sapphire, and King Solomon was believed to have used one to commune with God. An old Persian myth tells that the Earth sat on a giant sapphire which gave the sky its brilliant blue colour. In Buddhism, sapphire is known as the 'stone of the stones' because of its connection with the qualities of devotion, happiness, spiritual enlightenment and tranquillity. Due to its highly soothing and balancing effect, sapphire is beneficial for treating nervous conditions such as panic attacks, anxiety and stress. Labelled the 'Gem of the Heavens', sapphire was believed to bestow its wearer with strengthened vision, including prophetic visions of the future. It is a symbol of truth and constancy. Sapphires (especially star sapphires *) are good stones to work with to improve your psychic faculties or astral travel, stimulating the Third Eye chakra to enhance psychic experiences. Sapphire is also effective at stimulating the Crown Chakra, and is excellent for improving mental focus and clarity.

* Star Sapphire - A certain type of sapphire, containing a six-rayed star, caused by the presence of a radiating pattern of needle-like formations within the stone.

AQUARIUS'S FEATURE CRYSTAL ★ AMETHYST

'The Spiritual and Psychic Stone'

An extremely well-known, common, easy-to-find and popular stone, this is the stone of spiritual power and psychic energy. It has a high ethereal vibration and is an extremely powerful and protective stone, particularly for those born in February and under the signs of Aquarius and Pisces. Amethyst is the birthstone for the month of February, and its name is derived from the Greek word *amethystos*, literally meaning "not intoxicated." Purple has long been considered a royal colour, so it is not surprising that amethyst has been so much in demand throughout history. Amethysts are featured in the English Crown Jewels and were also a favourite of Ancient Egyptian royalty. Leonardo da Vinci wrote that amethyst could dissipate evil thoughts and quicken the intelligence. This charming stone awakens and activates our higher awareness and psychic abilities. Amethyst has strong cleansing and healing powers, and its serenity assists with enhancing meditation and the reaching of higher states of consciousness. Connected with the Crown and Third Eye chakras, amethyst offers protection, wisdom, focus, power, access to Divine understanding, ethereal awareness, and increases psychic abilities, healing and inner peace. Its best known use is for heightening and enhancing one's spiritual connections and insights; it can even open doors to other dimensions, planes and realities.

The radiation of violet light issuing from amethyst has been placed on record as providing a calming influence upon the nerves, making it balancing and comforting to the wearer, and is said to be instrumental in slowing rapid and agitated bodily movements, and helpful in easing neuralgia, headaches, gout and stress-related insomnia. Amethyst can be worn on parts of the upper body to encourage conversations with your higher self, and is especially beneficial when worn over the throat or heart. Encouraging selflessness, intuition, spiritual wisdom and Divine visualisation, amethyst can transmute Earthly energies to the higher vibrations of etheric realms. As a stone of tranquillity and contentment, it can also dispel anger, irritability, mood swings, fear and negativity. Amethyst can act as a compassionate anchor and ensures that you are emanating your energy from a place of peace and understanding. Wear or use some of this beautiful purple-hued stone to elevate you to higher places today! After all, your dreams are waiting for you to join them up there ... it's high time to heed their call.

AQUARIAN POWER CRYSTALS

Around six thousand years ago, in ancient Mesopotamia, the Sumerians started studying precious stones and minerals, as well as the stars, with a view of improving their lives in many ways by probing the secrets and mysteries of the Universe. Their esoteric interests and knowledge were such that they began to grasp the general connections between the Earth and the heavens, or the Solar system as they knew it, and the functions of stones and minerals as a link between the two. Their method of making these connections was by colour (for example the Sun was allocated all yellow stones), as well as other spiritual links. The gemstones listed for the portion of your zodiac sign are given their status as your 'power crystals' due to the links that can be made between your primary planetary ruler/s and your mutable planetary ruler (listed last), and each stone's particular colour, chemical and mineral compositions, healing properties, and the number they are given (based on the Mohs scale of hardness: for example, diamond scores a perfect 10 out of 10), all of which combine to align with your planetary rulers. Working mindfully with your planet's special crystals is one way you can increase the flow of power and magic into your life.

POWER CRYSTALS FOR FIRST HALF AQUARIANS ★ (20 January - 3 February)

Influenced by Uranus, Saturn and Mercury
Peridot, Brazilianite, Aventurine, Onyx, Wulfenite

PERIDOT ★ This crystal belongs to the olivine family and displays a charming range of greens, from pale to dramatic. The deep olive green coloured peridot, which has yellow lights radiating from its depths and is completely transparent, albeit sometimes with a slightly cloudy surface, is the most appropriate for those born in the second half of Aquarius. Peridot is an unusual stone in that it is the only gem found in meteorites. In ancient times, peridot was revered as a stone of purity that protected against negative energies. The pharaohs of ancient Egypt considered peridot to be the property of their gods, and it was traditionally used to keep evil spirits away. It is still considered, and used as, a protective stone and is beneficial to the aura. A power cleanser and tonic, it releases and neutralises toxins on all levels and purifies the mind and body. It opens, cleanses and activates the Heart and Solar Plexus chakras and clears burdens, bitterness, greed, guilt, jealousies, obsessions, unhelpful thoughts and 'baggage'. Peridot works well as an inspirational stone. When you feel stuck or blocked in a situation, use this crystal to help give you a fresh angle or insight into the solution. Peridot assists you to move forward, detach yourself from outside influences, and encourages you to look to your own higher energies for spiritual guidance. An effective mind-sharpener, it aids in learning how to forgive yourself and to step forth and take responsibility for your own life. It enhances confidence and assertion, and alleviates resentment, envy, anger, spite and hurts from the past. A generally revitalising and energising stone, it can help to banish lethargy, apathy and exhaustion. Mentally, it motivates growth and enhances transformation through making necessary changes in your life and promotes overall psychological wellbeing, clarity and ultimately, spiritual truth. It accelerates personal growth and enhances a feeling of inner joy and lightness, opening you up to giving, receiving and expressing this feeling. Peridot is a visionary crystal, which helps you to discover your destiny and your spiritual purpose, making it an excellent working stone for healers - and of course for the naturally far-sighted Aquarian spirit.

BRAZILIANITE ★ As its names suggests, this precious stone is found in Brazil (and the USA) and is an attractive bright yellow to yellowish-green gem. Brazilianite, resonating with the Solar Plexus and Sacral chakras, embodies a potent energy and profound vibration, enhancing creative abilities and guiding our journeys into past lives. This golden stone can cleanse your current life's past and re-empower you spiritually. Its stimulation of the Solar Plexus chakra can help aid manifestation and its loving heart-based energy can help increase your personal power, especially if used with focused intention and integrity. Its hardness (5 out of 10) and colour align it with Mercury's energy.

AVENTURINE ★ Coming in hues of green, blue, yellow, red, pink and glowing sunset, Aventurine is a unique member of the quartz family and owes its fine gold-speckled appearance to tiny flakes of mica or hematite in its body. Green is its most common colouring and this variety is considered the 'opportunity, chance and luck stone', and is the type of Aventurine I will focus on here. Connected with the Heart chakra, green Aventurine helps activate, clear and protect the heart, and is generally useful for treating heart problems on account of its ability to strengthen and stabilise the heart, as well as encourage regeneration of this vital organ - both physically and emotionally. A stone of comfort, balance and tranquillity, green Aventurine is favoured by healers who wish to promote wholeness and harmony. Aventurine's name is derived from the Italian for 'chance' or 'random', and it helps us to recognise opportunities and is said to place us exactly where we need to be for good things to transpire, as energetically it opens our mind to increased perception and creative insights, so that we are better able to recognise favourable circumstances. Aventurine encourages leadership, decisiveness, compassion, empathy, creativity and perseverance, and defuses negative situations and emotions. It also promotes new growth, optimism, and is an attractor of luck, wealth and prosperity - it is a traditional gambler's talisman. Aventurine has long enjoyed a reputation as a powerful manifestor of abundance; it works by drawing the energising strength of the Sun down to Earth to power this manifestation and attract prosperity. Aventurine is a stone of comfort and balance, encourages regeneration, opens the heart and restores trust, so is an excellent stone for those who find it difficult to open up their hearts to giving and receiving love. Green Aventurine will assist you to move on from a limited vision of your capabilities, and, encouraging exploration, it is helpful in career assessment or changes. Overall, Aventurine, and particularly green Aventurine, is an all-round healer, stimulating wellbeing, joy and calm, and enables you to live within your own centre.

ONYX ★ Onyx is a type of agate of various colours, sometimes black or white. Deriving its name from the Arabic 'el jaza' means sadness, onyx used to have a bad reputation as it was thought to make people pessimistic, lonely and sad, but amongst the virtues ascribed to it were those of protection - through avoiding conflicts, adversity and tragedy - and that of bringing patience and wisdom to those who wore it. Onyx is a grounding stone which has the ability to manipulate energy. It can be protective, but can also be used for more sinister purposes. It is ultimately a giver of strength and can restore depleted energies that have been taken from you. Its properties are Earthy and cooling, and it is well-suited to the energies of its planetary ruler, Saturn, which governs, order, discipline and structure. Saturn lends these qualities to onyx and therefore the stone's grounding nature makes it a good aid for solving matters that require solidity and determination. Onyx is well known for its use as a protective amulet, and is helpful in times where you may encounter negative influences, hostility or unpleasant people or environments. Because it absorbs negative forces however, it is important to cleanse this crystal after use, to avoid it holding the negative energies it has absorbed.

POWER CRYSTALS FOR SECOND HALF AQUARIANS ★ (4 - 18 February)

Influenced by Uranus, Saturn and Venus
Star Diopside, Tugtupite, Jade, Casiterite, Charoite, Torbetine

STAR DIOPSIDE ★ The resplendent Star Diopside can display a four-rayed hovering star with two sharp and two muted lines, hanging suspended over an almost opaque black-green to brownish-black body. Possibly the only top grade magnetic gemstone, Star Diopside contains needle-like crystals of magnetite that add to its beauty. Star Diopside is usually black, and when polished en cabochon, show's a cat's eye or star; it is therefore sometimes referred to as 'black star'. During the times of Atlantis and Lemuria, star Diopside was used as a scrying stone, so it will take you into the depths. It provides a great deal of protection for those exploring deep spiritual paths, and will keep you connected to the Earth while journeying or travelling the Universe. Indeed, it provides a link to otherworld entities and is excellent for exploring past lives. An excellent grounding stone for those undertaking astral travel, it can be used in combination with green barite for purging any unwanted entities you may encounter which are almost beings in themselves. Star Diopside can act as a protective shield during these explorations, and will absorb any excess energies that are cluttering the mind. Diopside assists you to remain detached and objective, stimulates the intellect and clears blocked emotions. When a decision needs to be made, consult a star Diopside. Gaze into its shining surface and see the star within - which is actually *you*. It has a hardness of 5.5, placing it in the vicinity of Venus's 6. Its beauty aligns it with Venus's vibrations, its colour with Saturn, and its surprising and unusual appearance with Uranus.

JADE ★ Two crystals are commonly known as jade by the gem trade: jadeite and nephrite. Although nephrite and jadeite are two distinct minerals with different holistic values, they do share many similarities. Jadeite was recognised as a separate mineral in 1863 by a French chemist, who analysed two separate specimens from China and found them to be different minerals. Since nephrite was firmly established, he called the second specimen jadeite. Jadeite's colours range through green, white, pink, black, yellow and mauve, with green being probably the most well-known. The most sought-after colouring is an intense apple green, an eye-catching, extremely rare and highly attractive gem also known as Imperial Jade. Jade brings peace through serenity and cleanses the energy centres. Green jade strengthens the Heart chakra and can be used to harmonise dysfunctional relationships. It calms the nervous system and channels passion in constructive ways. It increases love and nurturing and symbolises harmony, purity, serenity, protection, good luck and friendship. It is a serenity stone and is excellent for healing conditions associated with stress and feelings of overwhelming obligation. A wonderful ally in healing others, Jade is a good stone for those who are beginner healers or who wish to give their healing skills an added boost. The ancients considered Jade a sacred stone and it was traditionally worn as a stone of good fortune. On a spiritual level Jade has an affinity for the Heart chakra and it harmonises relationships, encourages compassion and the establishment of strong bonds, and balances the nervous system, dispelling moods swings and calming anger and irritability. It brings serenity when it is worn, carried or used, and instils wisdom, promotes feelings of tranquillity, cleanses feelings and stabilises the personality. Jade has a long history of being used to attract wealth and prosperity due to its associations with royalty. Chinese business people have long used jade to attract new business and promote worthy causes and ventures. Placing a piece of jade in your work space is beloved to attract wealth, and enhance calm and harmony in the work environment. Used with other stones or on its own, it is traditionally believed to generate abundance and attract good fortune in all areas of life. Jade is also a useful 'dream' stone; placed under your pillow, it encourages insightful dreams and will help you to not only remember your dreams, but also to interpret them. In addition, as a stone of wisdom, it assists us to reach decisions about meaningful things. Spiritually, jade encourages you to become who you really are. Awakening hidden knowledge within yourself, it assists in recognising yourself as a spiritual being on a human journey. A profoundly spiritual stone, jade encourages you to recognise that you have access to much wider powers and dimensions than can be physically seen, and motivates you to become all that you can be. It can also assist your understanding of any blocks which may be hindering manifestation or progress of your goals. Jade has the wonderful attribute of dispelling all negativity and indeed has been considered a sacred stone by various cultures for many centuries. The Chinese call jadeite 'Yu Shih' meaning Yu stone, believing it to contain all five cardinal virtues needed for a happy existence: modesty, courage, charity, justice and wisdom. Maori greenstone jade is a master healer and powerful manifestor.

CHAROITE ★ This is an expensive stone that is only found in one location in Russia, and its rarity makes it hard to come by. Its colours include pink, lilac, lavender, violet and vivid purple. Having a particular affinity for the Third Eye, Crown and Heart chakras, it allows us to connect with the spiritual dimensions while still remaining grounded. One of the most highly evolved mineral healers of the purple ray, Charoite accelerates spiritual growth by clearing emotional and mental blocks which are preventing you from changing your attitude. If you are resisting change, Charoite will assist in breaking through the barriers. Charoite is a stone of transformation, a soulful gem which stimulates inner vision, spiritual wisdom and vibrational change. It enhances your ability to be loving and generous and encourages a path of service to humanity, making it an ideal stone for the global-minded Aquarian. Charoite also alleviates deep fears, compulsions, obsessions and frustrations, and enhances drive, vigour, perspective, acceptance of others and unconditional love. Furthermore, it encourages deep, peaceful sleep and bestows powerful dreams, while at the same time warding off nightmares. It has the ability to transform fear into insight and eases emotional turmoil. This stone, if you can find one, is a magical and mysterious dream-fulfiller with the ability to transform and manifest our deepest desires. A stone of prophecy, Charoite assists us in understanding our visions. Violet-coloured crystals such as Charoite will help take you into a fantasy world, in which you can create or alter your reality. They can open the doors to other realms, release our fears, and remove obstacles from our paths. Charoite is ultimately a cleanser and transmuter of negativity, clearing the aura and chakras, raising our self-esteem, and enabling us to express our unconditional love by opening up our hearts and spirits.

YOUR LUCKY NUMBERS

Your lucky numbers are ★ 5 for Aquarius ^, 4 for Uranus & 8 for Saturn (your traditional ruler) (also, see 'Lucky Magic Square of Saturn')

LUCKY MAGIC SQUARE OF SATURN

In Western occult tradition, each planet has traditionally been associated with a series of numbers and particular arrangements of those numbers. One such method of numerological organisation is the magic square. Magic squares date back to ancient times, appearing in China about 3,000 years ago. The first Chinese square is seen in the scroll of the river Lo - the Lo-Shu, a scroll believed to have been created by Fuh-Hi, the mythical founder of Chinese civilisation. Certain squares came to be linked with the planets; these associations came from the Babylonians. Each *kamea*, or magic square, is linked with a particular planet, and each of the squares has a *seal*, which is the geometric pattern created by following the numbers in order of their value. This pattern touches upon all the numbers of the square and the seal is used to represent the entire square. An intelligence and a spirit are also associated with each kamea, derived from the key numbers contained within it, using a Hebrew form of numerology. This intelligence is viewed as an inspiring, guiding and informing entity.

The 'Magic Square of Saturn' is divided into 9 cells, or squares, three across and three down. The sum of the numbers in the vertical, horizontal and diagonal lines is a constant of 15. The total of these numbers is 45. Therefore, the numbers 3, 9, 15 and 45 are also assigned to Saturn.

YOUR NUMEROLOGY NUMBER & LUCKY SUN SIGN NUMBERS

"Everything that exists has a vibration. The vibration of sound, music, colour, matter, even our words, thoughts, and names show form. All vibration is measurable. To measure we need numbers. Numbers are the basis of all. Numbers are the key to all mysteries."
Shirley Blackwell Lawrence, *Behind Numerology*

Numerology is essentially the metaphysical * 'science' of numbers. The use of numbers in magic is its cornerstone of power. The ancient Greek philosopher and mathematician Pythagoras, born around 590 BC, embarked on a thirty-year spiritual quest studying with important religious and esoteric teachers and healers to find the mystery of 'The Hidden Light', and came to see mankind as living in three worlds: the natural, the human and the Divine. He asserted that all things can be expressed in numerical terms, because they are ultimately reducible to numbers. Pythagoras stated that "Numbers are the first things of all of Nature" and followed the theory that "Nothing can exist without numbers."

Many believe that numbers have an arcane, mystical relationship with words, and with inanimate and animate objects; the interpretations that arose from these relationships date back to a time when the dawning intelligence of primitive man first visualised the meaning of numbers and associated it with spiritual significance. Numerology is the science of the exploration of this relationship in order to discover hidden meanings, forecast the future or interpret the character of a person. In its more modern applications, a series of figures which correspond to an individual's name and date of birth are calculated, and practitioners believe one's prospects, fortune and character can be deciphered from the results ^.

So what is numerology and how does one use it? Everything in the Universe has a vibrational frequency, an energy, a force, all vibrating at various rates, and we as humans are no exception, the difference between one person and another is their rate of vibration. This force or energy is constantly in motion and changing, and we can even 'tune into' and feel our vibrations if we are still for long enough.

Along with letters, sounds, colours, crystals, and many other things, it is believed that numbers also have vibrations, and when we are able to familiarise ourselves with our own numerical frequencies, we can use this familiarity to add power and magic to our lives. The numbers of our birth date, the letters of our names, and the numbers of our Sun sign and ruling planets, all have a unique vibrational frequency, and herein lies the key to understanding our self and our journey through life. Numerology refers to the knowledge contained within the numbers of our birth date and our name, and this is our own personal magic which can greatly assist us through life.

* Metaphysics is the study of those sciences that extend beyond the physical or tangible

HOW TO FIND YOUR NUMEROLOGY NUMBER

^ Your Sun sign's number was added up according to the principle of corresponding a number with a letter, for example 1=A, 2=B, 3=C and so on in sequence and up to 9=I, then beginning again at number 1 for the next letter J and following this same sequence. Following this system, the sum of the letters in Aquarius vibrates to the number 5.

Your personal numerology number is determined by adding up all the numbers in your birth date until they reach a two-digit figure. The two resulting numbers are then added together again to form a single digit, which is your personal numerology number. For example, someone born on 3 February 1983, would add the digits 3 + 2 + 1 + 9 + 8 + 3 = 26 = (reduced to two digits) 8. So that person's personal numerology birth number is 8.

Each primary number or birth number from 1 to 9 has a specific meaning and is governed by a planetary force. The principle of numerology reduces all numbers down to the following: 1 to 9, and 10, 11, 13 and 22 *. The last four numbers only apply to people specially concerned with the occult and spiritualism - and can be studied at greater length through other sources if so desired - and can in any case be reduced further to a single digit if preferred.

Your birth number contains a unique power, and therein lie your strengths, shortcomings and opportunities. It is beyond the scope of this book to outline your individual numerology number possibilities, so for the purposes of astrological applications, I have only included your Sun sign and ruling planet's special numbers.

* The numbers 10 and 13, and the master numbers 11 and 22, can be further reduced to one digit if so desired; however, they can be interpreted as they are without further reduction. The choice is personal.

BASIC MEANINGS & KEYWORDS

1 ★ Sun. Masculine influence, beginnings, independence, inventiveness, originality, leadership, exploration, innovation, ambition
2 ★ Moon. Feminine influence, cooperation, partnership, tact, diplomacy, harmony, unity, emotions, imagination, adaptability
3 ★ Jupiter. Communication, expression, youthfulness, self-confidence, creativity, inspiration, optimism, curiosity
4 ★ Uranus. Order, form, security, stability, patience, restriction, work, values, practicality
5 ★ Mercury. Freedom, inconsistency, change, variety, travel, activity, learned
6 ★ Venus. Love, home, family, sense of duty, responsibility, marriage, justice, nurturing, balance, gentleness, peace, friendship

7 ★ Neptune. Analysis, wisdom, mystical, spiritual, solitude, precision, research, integrity, mystery, psychic perceptions

8 ★ Saturn. Money, power, success, organisation, hard work, business, health, purpose, control, authority, mastery

9 ★ Mars. Completion, endings, Universal, service, humanity, philanthropy, loyalty

10 ★ Fortunate, creative, vibrant, stable, optimistic, original, successful, determined, individualistic

11 ★ Master number. Prophecies, inspiration, moral courage, missionary, long-suffering, foolhardiness, enlightenment, invention

13 ★ Misunderstood, fearful, changeable, interested in the occult, fatalistic, flexible, sacred, beguiling

22 ★ Master number. Powerful, successful, idealistic, attracted to the occult, creative, wise, successful, masterful, spiritually understanding

★ THE NUMBER 4 - FOR URANUS ★

Names ★ Quartet, Quadruple, Quart, Quaternary

Arithmomantic connections with the letters of the alphabet ★ D, M and V

Ruled by Uranus, which brings efficiency, industriousness and practicality to those born under its influence, the number 4 can be rather dull, and lack imagination, emotions and empathy. Four is the number is stability, providing physical structure, balance and integrity. The Quaternary, the number 4, or the Tetrad, was regarded by many ancients as symbolic of truth, while the Greeks considered it to be the root of all things. Traditionally the number of the Earth - there are four seasons and four primal elements (Fire, Earth, Air, Water) - four can be said to represent many other things also: the four liberal sciences were considered to be astronomy, geometry, music and arithmatic, four accepted states of death, judgement, heaven and hell, four compass point directions, four winds, four Archangels guarding the Earth (Uriel, Michael, Raphael and Gabriel) and four humours (phlegmatic, melancholic, choleric and sanguine), four limbs of the human body, Four Noble Truths (in Buddhism), the perfect number according to Pythagoras, being the source of ten ($1 + 2 + 3 + 4 = 10$), and significantly, the four suits of the Minor Arcana (Wands, Swords, Pentacles, Cups) - the number four brings structure and order, which is demonstrated perfectly in the square, an equal-sided, balanced, stable and dependable shape.

It is the number of reality, logic and reason. The essence of man's threefold nature - mind, body and spirit - is brought to the material plane, to form a square, symbolising reality and solidity. Four is an unlikely number for Uranus, for this is the number of will, purpose, construction and discipline - and does not like the boat being rocked, unlike Uranus itself. Number 4s are the planners and constructors of life, how love to pore over numbers and lists, columns and details. Number 4 - the number of the seasons, the elements, the points of the compass - is oriented to the Earth, and its subjects are usually steady and practical, with great endurance. Yet number 4 - the square - contains its own opposite, and number 4 people often see everything from the *opposite* point of view, making them seem rebellious and unconventional. And because you are so sure of yourself in practical situations, you are inclined to boss others around and believe you know best. If feeling discouraged, you can slip into melancholia. You are rarely interested in material things, and making friends is hard for you, so you may often feel isolated. Tending to see things in black and white, you may also lack vivid imagination, but if you are in an environment of gentle music, soothing colours, quiet activities and overall calm, clearly defined structure, you always come out of your shell to shine. Sunday is your special day.

Alchemy ★ Four stands for the four elements of Earth, Water, Fire and Air, the 'building blocks' of creation. Four signifies two sets of polarities, but although this creates tension, this tension can be used to create a house, for example, or lay out an arena for action. It can also create an enclosed area such as a philosophical rose garden. There are always battles where four is involved, but there is also potential for constructive work. The usual representation of four is the cross or the square.

LUCKY 'MAGIC HOURS' OR 'TIME UNITS'

One rule of magic, luck and power, as already outlined elsewhere in this book, can be found within the well-known phrase, "As above, so below." From the most ancient times, the planets were said to rule Earthly destinies and powers. Days of the week were named after the seven planets which were the only ones then known: Sun Day, Moon Day, Mars Day (French: Mardi), Mercury Day (French: Mercredi), Jove Day (French: Jeudi), Venus Day (French: Vendredi) and Saturn Day.

The planetary hours are based on an ancient astrological system, the Chaldean order of the planets. The Chaldean order indicates the relative orbital velocity of the planets, and from a heliocentric (helios = The Sun) perspective, this sequence also indicates the relative distance of the planets from the Sun (the Sun switching places with the Earth in this sequence), and the distance of the Moon from the Earth.

Before an action is taken in daily life, or a transaction undertaken, for instance, it is possible to choose the appropriate day and hour that will provide the greatest chances of success. By studying the planetary hours system, you will discover which actions are propitious to which of the seven planets or 'star-gods' and at what time it would be advisable to undertake them.

The planetary hours system uses this Chaldean order to divide time, and each planetary hour of the planetary day is ruled by a different planet. The order is repeated, starting with the slowest: Saturn - then, Jupiter, Mars, Sun, Venus, Mercury, Moon, then back to Saturn, Jupiter, Mars, etc., ad infinitum. The planet that rules the first hour of the day is also the ruler of that whole day and gives the day its name. So the first hour of Saturday is ruled by Saturn, the first hour of Sunday by the Sun, and so on. It is important, for the purposes of using specific planetary energies for our magic and wishes, to note that planetary hours are not considered the same length as our normal time-keeping slots of sixty minutes. Each day is split into time periods, day time and night time, beginning at around sunrise and sunset respectively. These two time periods are each divided into twelve equal-length hours, which are the planetary hours. So the planetary hours of the day and the planetary hours of the night will be of different lengths, except during the equinoxes when light and darkness are balanced.

In sequence, the Sun, Moon and the five visible planets each exerts its own special influence over a twenty-four-hour period. I like to call your planet's special day and hour the 'Magic Hour'.

Magic rituals to draw luck and love to you should be conducted at astrologically correct times and with the appropriate instruments, tools, cards, herbs, flowers, oils and plants which are linked with the ruling planet. For example, a love ritual, spell or potion demands a concoction of any or all of the above ruled by Venus. Do not underestimate rulerships, for they wield an unseen power that can help make our dreams, big and small, come true.

Further, as specific hours of each day are ruled by certain planets, if you are really serious about attracting some power, luck or magic into your life, it is imperative that you wish, pray or ask at the most opportune times for your Sun sign. There are two methods you can use for fine tuning your magical workings. The first method is to perform your spell, ritual or wishing on the day your Sun sign's ruling planet during the planetary hour that signifies the essence of what you are asking for (e.g. An Aquarius who is looking for love might perform a love-seeking ritual on a Saturday, during a Venus-ruled planetary hour). Alternatively, if you wish to summon the power of your Sun sign's own ruling planet, then that same Aquarian might perform their love-seeking ritual on a Friday (ruled by Venus) during Saturn's planetary hour.

The nature of that which you are asking for, such as love, travel opportunities, money, career guidance, protection or friendship for example, should always be considered when choosing the day or hour during which your magic will be heightened.

The answer to the question why are there seven days in a week, is a very important one to know in unravelling the secret of your Magic Hours. Ancient people recognised the supreme importance of the seven heavenly spheres, which comprised those which could be seen by the naked eye: The Sun, Moon, Mercury, Venus, Mars, Jupiter and Saturn. They then named each of the seven days of the week after one of those spheres and assigned that planetary 'ruler' to one day of the week. As viewed from Earth, these seven spheres appear to move at varying speeds, and the ancients used this factor to arrange them in order of varying speed. If you intend to use your Magic Hours to attract wonderful things, you must memorise that sequence because it is what forms the basis of the whole system.

Whenever you intend to use your Magic Hours or, perhaps more accurately, Magic *Time Units*, it is important to find out the exact time of sunrise for the area in which you live, as sunrise marks the time when your planet's magic is at its most powerful on its specific day. So, at sunrise on Sunday, the Sun rules the hour following the sunrise, the Moon rules the first hour following sunrise on a Monday, and through the week the pattern is repeated, with each day's ruling planet beginning the cycle in that first hour after dawn. It is logical then, that the rest of the planets, in sequence, follow on with one planet per hour for that day thereafter for the rest of the 24-hour cycle, creating a Magic Hour or Time Unit for each planet throughout the day and night, depending on which planet rules that particular day and is therefore the first in line.

If you wish to explore the idea in more depth, it is worth noting first and foremost that each day contains twenty-four hours, but, depending on the season, day and night will be of varying lengths. In summer, daylight is longer than darkness, whereas the reverse applies in winter. During autumn and spring, day and night are usually about equal. Therefore, although a complete day always contains twenty-four hours, there are not always twelve hours between sunrise and sunset and another twelve hours between sundown and the following sunrise. So, depending on the season (and location), a time unit may be shorter than one hour, longer than one hour, or equal to one hour. So whenever you intend to use your Magic Time Units, it is important to find out the exact time of sunrise and sunset for the area in which you live. The next step is to divide the amount of daytime (if day when you wish to work your 'magic', otherwise the same following theory applies to night time) into twelve equal sections by calculating the number of hours and minutes between sunrise and sunset and divide by twelve. An example is if the Sun rises at 6.27 a.m. and sets at 5.49 p.m., the amount of time contained in this day is eleven hours and twenty-two minutes. Convert this total into minutes (682) and then divide that figure by twelve (57). Therefore, each of the twelve daylight time units will be 57 minutes on that day.

Although this wonderful method of using astrology is very ancient, it may be completely new to you. You are in for a pleasant surprise though, because if you are willing to delve into a little research and put the system to the test, rich rewards are in store for you!

YOUR LUCKY DAY ★ SATURDAY

Planet ★ Saturn
Basic Energy ★ Restriction, Crossroads, Authority
Basic Magic ★ Banishing, Rewards, Wisdom
Element ★ Earth
Colours ★ Black or Midnight Blue
Energy Keywords ★ Caution, Responsibility, Rigidity, Sternness, Justice, Seriousness, Defence, Authority, Time, Fear, Humility, Law, Patience, Pessimism, Age, Respect, Sincerity, Restraint, Severity, Wisdom, Thrift

Saturday is the day of Saturn, your traditional (or secondary) ruler. In commonly used calendars, Saturday is the seventh day of the week, though in others it is the sixth. The Romans named Saturday *Saturni dies*, meaning 'Saturn's Day' no later than the 2nd century for the planet Saturn, which was believed to control the first hour of that day. Some cultures and religions observe Saturday as Shabbat or Sabbath, which stretches from sundown Friday to sundown Saturday and is the day of rest. Other religions distinguish between Saturday (Sabbath) and the Lord's Day (Sunday). Black Saturday, a day named after the beginning of tragic bushfires in Victoria Australia, Holy Saturday, the day before Easter, and Lazarus Saturday, the day before Palm Sunday which is part of the 'Holy Week', are some well-known examples with which Saturn's day is associated.

Saturday ends the week in most calendars, and is ruled by dark-browed Saturn, father of the gods and ruler of time. His help can be sought for anything to do with old age, and with establishing or breaking down boundaries, limitations and structures. His magic works slowly but although subtle it can be extremely powerful, if you have the patience to allow him to work with you on whatever you are wishing for.

In the folk rhyme 'Monday's Child', 'Saturday's child works hard for a living'. It is a day of Leadership, Ambition, Authority, Hard Work, Perseverance, Dedication, Responsibility and Duty, and an opportune day for making wishes or working magic involving long-term goals, careers, institutions, establishments, security, investments, karma, 'reversals', building structure, protection, solitude, privacy, determination, endings, blocking, renewing and transforming. Although these words are more aligned with Capricorn, as your modern ruler Uranus does not have rulership over any day of the week, Aquarians can still make good use of these activities and qualities given Saturn's co-rulership over their sign.

SATURN'S MAGIC TIME UNITS
(BASED ON THE PLANETARY HOURS)
FOR EACH DAY OF THE WEEK

SATURDAY ★ First and Eighth time units after sunrise
SUNDAY ★ Fifth and Twelfth time units after sunrise
MONDAY ★ Second and Ninth time units after sunrise
TUESDAY ★ Sixth time unit after sunrise
WEDNESDAY ★ Third and Tenth time units after sunrise
THURSDAY ★ Seventh time unit after sunrise

FRIDAY ★ Fourth and Eleventh time units after sunrise
**

Choose the Hour/s of Saturn to start a long-term project, build, construct, lay down the basis or foundation for an ambitious venture, ask for wise advice, enter into a long-term commitment, start a fundamental curative treatment, devote yourself to serious study, or to study a complicated dossier.

** Please note that for the purposes of simplification, the information regarding 'Saturn's Magic Time Units' is a very diluted and simplified version of using magical times to your advantage. These hours cover only daylight hours, or the first twelve hours after sunrise, and do not take into account magical times after sunset or throughout the night. 'Hours' is also a deceptive term, as most 'time periods' used in this system are less than an hour, but for the purposes of simplifying the technique, I refer to them as Magic Hours (to keep with the tradition of the term 'planetary hours') rather than magic 'time units', which is what they really are. Should you wish to do further research on your ruling planet's most powerful time units, or require further information about the planet/s from which you are seeking 'energy' from in order to assist your wish-making, other sources may provide you with more comprehensive and detailed information.

A LITTLE NEW MOON / MAGICAL TIME UNIT WISH RITUAL

Step 1 ~ Choose the Magical Hour and/or day that matches your intentions. The first dawn hour of Sunday, ruled by the Sun, is a great time for all-purpose magic, success, joy, abundance, prosperity, bliss, personal power & all-round expansion.

Step 2 ~ Write out a little wish list with the appropriate coloured pen on the colour paper which corresponds to your desire.

Step 3 ~ Choose a small stone of your choosing that is connected to your wish (or a number of stones, that are perhaps linked with your planetary ruler's number, for example 4 for Uranus).

Step 4 ~ Find a nice patch of soil in your garden or any special place to you, dig into it, affirm your wish in your mind, place the crystal/s and piece of paper in the hole, then place a plant on top of the crystal/s and wish list.

Step 5 ~ Fill the soil back in over the roots of the plant and feed it with a little water out of a magical vessel (a small genie bottle would be ideal).

Step 6 ~ Thank the Earth, the Universe and the Sun (or whatever planet you are summoning the power from) for bringing forth your desires.

Step 7 ~ Repeat all day long: "Thank You, Thank You, Thank You!"

Step 8 ~ Watch your plant - and your wish - grow bigger and bigger as time goes on!

YOUR LUCKY CHARM/TALISMANS

The following are three 'materials' or talismanic symbols from which to make your lucky charms, and the planetary energy under which to do it, corresponding with your Sun sign:

AQUARIUS ★ Amethyst, Key *, Lead, Saturn

"When any star ascends fortunately, take a stone and
herb that are under that star, make a ring of
the metal that is congruous therewith, and in that fix
the stone with the herb under it."
Henry Cornelius Agrippa, *On Occult Philosophy*

Charms, talismans and amulets are among the oldest forms of magic. A charm or talisman is a symbol, often used to communicate a thought, prayer or wish to, or to make a connection with the Divine. It is usually in the form of an object, which has been imbued with mysterious and magical powers. A charm may be as simple as a stone, a flower or a feather, or it might be a parchment bearing writing; the meaning and significance that you attribute to the symbol is what is important. It can be created by yourself (to best effect) or by someone else, and works as a tool to activate our subconscious mind.

You can use general charms such as a cross, or a universally lucky symbol such as a horseshoe, but you will exude and therefore attract more potency and protection if you make and wear the appropriate charms with the matching gemstone, set in the right metal and created under the corresponding planetary influence. While most people wear silver or gold, cheaper tin or copper may be more appropriate and indeed beneficial for your Sun sign. An amulet (for protection) or a talisman or charm (for luck), must also be made, ordered, designed or purchased on the appropriate day of the week for its power to be most effective. Your day, as previously described, is Saturday.

You can even go further and create or buy your amulet or charm at one of the hours and/or days when your planet is exerting its most powerful influence. It may sound complicated and requiring of forethought and effort, but if you are going to summon magic and are superstitious enough to truly *believe* that you can do this (and remember pure belief in something is the starting point of all manifestation), you should be scrupulous enough to do it properly. For your planet's day and time, please consult the information under the previous headings 'Your Lucky Day' and 'Saturn's Magic Time Units'.

* The Key ★ There are many superstitious beliefs around keys, the main one being that to wear one will attract good luck and fortune. This belief is at the root of the practice of giving keys to a young person as a coming-of-age gift so that they may have a life filled with blessings. Wearing three keys around your neck is thought to bring wealth, health and happiness. Putting a key near a baby's cot was once regarded as a protective symbol, to ward off fairies and keep them from putting a changeling in its place (this might be a reason why rattles and teething toys are often shaped like keys). Keys are phallic symbols, and in placing a key in a lock we are unconsciously calling upon the powers of Divine union and creation. As keys play a vital role in our security, their main role in magic is one of overall protection.

GODS, GODDESSES, ANIMAL TOTEMS & OTHER 'GUIDES'

Gods, goddesses and guides can be summoned to help you live your life to its optimal best. Some are connected with your Sun sign, while others may be of your own personal choosing, ones you may feel particularly drawn towards. Those which align with your ruling planet and your Sun sign, give a good indication of those who will shine a guiding light along your desired path, but you can choose your own too, based upon exploration, observations, research, meditation or simple intuition - I believe choosing your own, based on your inner *knowing* or guidance system, is a very powerful magical tool. However, to get you started, following are some animal spirit guide ideas for your contemplation. Good luck!

YOUR LUCKY ANIMALS & BIRDS

Dog, Vulture, Cuckoo, Peacock, Albatross, Phoenix, Owl, Eel, Crow, Large Birds Which Fly Afar, Otter

"Somewhere beyond the walls of our awareness … the wilderness side, the hunter side, the seeking side of ourselves is waiting to return."
Laurens van der Post, *The Heart of the Hunter*

"(People) everywhere are being made acutely aware of the fact that something essentially to life and wellbeing is flickering very low in the human species and threatening to go out entirely. This 'something' has to do with such values as love, unselfishness, sincerity, loyalty to one's best friend, honesty, enthusiasm, humility, goodness, happiness … fun. Practically every animal has these assets in abundance and is eager to share them, given the opportunity and the encouragement."
Jay Allen Boone, *Kinship with All Life*

Some astrological systems, such as Shamanistic * or Native American Astrology, tell us that the Sun sign we were born under has a corresponding animal totem, which informs us about our characteristics and act as a kind of spiritual guide or mentor throughout our life's journey. These totems are described as Solar totems, because many of them share similarities with the Solar system and the sign the Sun was passing through at the time of our birth, and therefore relate to animals and animal behaviours which also correspond to environmental conditions and seasonal changes. These animals encompass many aspects of the Solar system, from seasonal relationships, to creature instincts, to reciprocal links with the planetary vibrations, and 'clans' within nature that you are inherently closely connected with through your date of birth.

Carl Jung, a master of dream analysis and interpretation, proposed that animals symbolise our natural instincts, operating through our dreams. He theorised that certain dream symbols, among them animals, represent core emotions and concepts, archetypes that will hold true for all of us the world over, regardless of so-called 'divisions' such as sex, customs, age or culture. In *Man and His Symbols*, Jung states that primitive societies believed that each person had a bush soul and a human soul. The bush soul incarnates as a tree or animal - a totem - and when the bush soul is harmed or injured, the human soul is considered injured as well.

Some of the most important and powerful spirit guides are those belonging to the animal kingdom. Both in ancient times and in some traditional modern tribal systems, people consult with animals for their wisdom and personal power. Even though most societies today have drifted away from this connection, it has never really left us, and different creatures continue to communicate with us on both the physical and spiritual planes in an attempt to speak to our souls and spirits.

As part of the teaching world, animals can bring us wisdom and survival skills, while others show us how to adapt, transcend or morph. Others still can remind us the importance of play and humour, and guide us around how to overcome life's challenges. Many are known for their loyalty and ability to love unconditionally and without judgement, while some have a grounded and healthy detachment, remaining true to themselves rather than pleasing others, an important lesson in itself. Whatever the qualities of the unique animal guides for your Sun sign, all have some enlightening soul-awakening traits that can teach us much about our own true inner selves. Ultimately, your animal spirit guides, and in particular your Solar totem animal, endow you with qualities that will enhance your life and help to activate your creativity, wisdom and intuition, helping to heal the broken or return the lost pieces of your soul and reconnect you to the natural world.

Your Solar totem animal (listed last on your lucky birds and animals list) is not the same as an animal spirit guide, which is based on metaphysical principles and is also based on your soul's mission in this embodiment - however, you can definitely make your birth Solar totem animal your spiritual guide if you wish, as you may find that its qualities, traits, symbolism and messages strongly reflect and define your own nature - or what you aspire to become, manifest or draw towards you. Your birth totem power animal comes from a place of trust and innocence, and represents the essence of your creative inner child. If you spend some time meditating on your Solar totem animal, asking what lessons it can teach, and reflect deeply on its character, life and habits, you may find it connects with you on a deep spiritual level and you can make the necessary changes to your life to draw in more magic and power.

Overall, if your life is stagnant or in need of healing or an energy boost, you can request your animal spirit or spirits to come and help you change your vibration, awaken your truth and arouse your inner forces. If you are aware of your animal spirit's presence in your life every day, you can use its particular energies to support, guide and teach you. And above all, pay attention to any signs and expressions of its lessons, and remember to thank your chosen animal guide for helping you.

* Shamanism is a traditional spiritual practice of the Native American culture. A shaman, one who practices this age-old art, is an intermediary between the human world and the world of the spirits. He inherits his magical powers at birth, but spends many years as an apprentice, so that he is usually much older in age before he is able to practice and call upon his skills. People ask for a shaman's help when there is a crisis on either a personal or wider spread scale, such as famine, drought, war or illness. The shaman makes contact with the spirits by going into a trance. First, he may perform a series of rituals, which usually include drumming, singing and chanting, and when these have brought on the right conditions, he leaves his body behind to travel to the other world. There he meets with the spirits of his ancestors, who inform him what must be done to relieve the suffering of his people. If the shaman is asked to cure someone of a dis-ease, then the spirits may accompany him to find the correct medicinal herbs or treatments for his patient.

YOUR FEATURE ANIMAL ★ OTTER

The Otter's Message ★ The application of spiritual knowledge, play, fun and wisdom to daily Earthly life. If you go with the natural ebbs and flows of life, you will discover joy, wonder and simple pleasures
Brings the totem gift of ★ Perception, inventiveness, playfulness and original thinking
Shares the power energies of ★ Tolerance, courage, originality, invention and exuberance
Brings forth and teaches the magic of ★ Creativity, the attaining of wisdom, the acquisition of knowledge, and the value of play, imagination, spontaneity and joy

    Being a water creature, the otter's symbolism is linked to the Divine and primal feminine, its watery habitat symbolising water as the giver and elixir of life. As the Solar totem and spirit animal guide for the Water Bearer, the otter can remind Aquarians of the importance of play, good-natured rough handling, frolicking, laughter, pure joy and spontaneous, spirited romps with others. Having few enemies in the wild, the otter can also impart lessons in feelings of wellbeing, security and fearlessness. Joyful, agile and nimble, the otter represents agility, curiosity, energy, dexterity, creativity and playfulness. Further, otters are commonly regarded as lucky animals. They feature as light-hearted tricksters in most folklore, and although their exploits are mischievous, they are generally not considered malicious or aggressive.

    The Otter is linked with the Moon, and because of this it has been used in initiation and fertility ceremonies in certain cultures. There is a belief among the North American Indians that the otter has been granted special powers, so some shamans use otter-skin bags in initiation rituals.

If you are feeling a little depleted in energy or enjoyment, try calling upon the otter to enliven your soul and restore your spirit. It might even stir you to dance with life and will almost definitely loosen you up and help to re-program the value of play. The more serious side of the otter is that they can be a little quirky and unorthodox, making the otter sometimes difficult to figure out. Although unconventional and misunderstood, the otter's methods are usually very effective. The otter may have an odd way of doing, expressing or perceiving things, but is blessed with a brilliant imagination and intelligence, giving him/her an edge over all others. Perceptive, friendly, intuitive, dynamic, sharing and attentive, the otter may be rebellious at times, but is also truthful, loyal, sympathetic and courageous. Through the otter we learn the courage to open up through play, to surrender to the trust that our needs will always be met, and to experience the bliss of pure and simple pleasures.

SPIRITUAL KEEPER ★ BUFFALO

Your spiritual keeper guides your spiritual growth and brings illumination. Your spiritual keeper is determined by the season in which you were born. Regarded as the 'keepers' or 'caretakers' of the Universe, the four Directions or alignments were also referred to by the Native Americans as the Four

Winds because their presence was *felt* rather than seen. The Direction to which your birth time belongs influences the nature of your inner senses. The North Direction's totem is the Buffalo. The Buffalo is a symbol of the mind and its sustenance - knowledge. The Buffalo (or Bison) is a revered symbol and a mighty albeit confronting animal, each beast weighing up to a tonne. It teaches us the gifts of provision, gratitude, abundance, prosperity, blessing, stability, consistency and strength. Its medicine includes manifestation, protection, Earth creativity, courage, knowledge, generosity, sharing, and giving for the greater good. The Buffalo brings you the endurance and power to walk the Great Road of pure intent that leads to happiness, health and fulfilment, bringing the sustenance that offers renewal and rebirth after a long, arduous winter. The power of the North's influence is primarily with the mind and wisdom, and the specific influence of this direction on Buffalo people is on intuitive sense, enabling you to Divine hidden truths, and endowing you with a deep sensitivity both to others' feelings and to mystical matters. Having this animal as your spiritual keeper bestows you with the gifts of a clear and keen mind, a quiet wisdom, and the power of renewing your energies from your own inner resources. The Buffalo is a reminder of the greater whole and its symbolism illustrates, in magical ways, the interconnectedness of everything in the world - and the wider Universe. Your animal keeper the Buffalo is, above all, a potent symbol of oneness and abundance.

CLAN ★ BUTTERFLY

Your clan animal comes from a place of inner knowing and intuition, helping you to discover the essence and magic of your true self. The Butterfly, a totem of the Air clan, represents and protects all that is beautiful and holds the secrets of change and personal transformation. The Butterfly symbolises that this transformation is always available to you, and may even begin without your conscious participation. Butterfly *is* the power of Air, the ability to float along on a breeze, and to 'dance' from place to place. They awaken our sense of lightness and joy, and teach us to dance with life rather than take it too seriously. In the folklore of some tribes, butterflies stand for change and balance, while in others ephemeral beauty, and some believe it to be symbolic of vanity and frivolity. Many tribes consider butterflies to be symbols of good luck, and some associate them with sleep and dreaming, decorating cradleboards and other children's items to help induce calm sleep and bring pleasant dreams. Butterflies symbolise metamorphosis, teaching us to trust in the process of change, re-awaken us to joy, and teach us that life is full of surprises and to therefore live with a constant sense of passion, intensity and wonder.

YOUR CORRESPONDING CHINESE ASTROLOGY ANIMAL

The Chinese Zodiac, known as Sheng Xiao (literally meaning 'birth likeness'), is based on a twelve-year cycle, each year in that cycle related to a particular animal. These animals are: Rat, Ox, Tiger, Rabbit, Dragon, Snake, Horse, Sheep, Monkey, Rooster, Dog and Pig. The selection and order of the animals that so influence people's lives, particularly in East Asian cultures, originated in the Han Dynasty (202 BC - 220 AD) and was based upon each animal's traits, characteristics, tendencies and living habits. Further, ancient people observed that there were twelve Full Moons in a year, and that, among other similarly related celestial observations, suggests its origins are also based on astronomical concepts.

The legend of the Chinese zodiac's story usually begins with the Jade Emperor, or Buddha (depending on who is telling the tale), summoning all the animals of the Universe for a race or a banquet. The twelve animals of the zodiac all appeared at the palace, and the order in which they arrived determined the order of the Chinese zodiac.

Each oriental animal corresponds with a Western astrology sign. For Aquarius, it is the Tiger.

> "I am the delightful Paradox.
> All the world is my stage.
> I set new trails ablaze;
> I seek the unattainable,
> And try the untried.
> I dance to life's music
> In gay abandon.
> Come with me on my carousel rides.
> See the myriads of colours,
> The flickering lights.

All hail me the unparalleled performer.
I am the Tiger."
Theodora Lau

Chinese name for the Tiger ★ HU
Ranking Order ★ Third
Hours ruled by the Tiger ★ 3 a.m. to 5 a.m.
Direction ★ East - Northeast
Season and principle month ★ Winter - February
Corresponds to the Western sign ★ Aquarius

★ **TIGER** ★ *Fixed Element Wood*

★ **Keywords** ★

Sensitive, short-tempered, brave, impetuous, lucky, playful, tireless, magnetic, hesitant, authoritative, indecisive, makes poor decisions, courageous, hasty, disobedient, proud

The Tiger is the third animal of the Chinese horoscope. As the name of this magnificent creature implies, there is a lot of speed, power and movement present in your nature. In fact, Tiger types are quite hasty and passionate, sometimes even hot-headed and unpredictable. Traditionally a yang animal, Tigers are generous, courageous, dynamic, liberal and active. Possessing magnetic personalities, the Tiger is a masculine sign and those born during its years tend to be generous and brave. People tend to follow your lead and you have the power to influence, because your commanding personality and expansive innovative style inspire confidence. You dislike feeling confined or bored, and can be rash, brash, proud and authoritative. You are usually competitive and like to win; somehow luck seems to be your friend. Certainly you are often found in positions of power, unless your desire for mobility and novelty urges you to move forward.

YOUR METALS

Aquarian power metals are Uranium, Platinum, Lead and Aluminium.

Although the magic power of crystals is widely recognised and applied, the influence radiating from metals is often overlooked. Metal, too, emits a powerful energy and in fact, in Chinese philosophy, metal is considered so essential and powerful that it is classified as one of the elements, alongside Air, Fire, Earth and Water.

As already mentioned earlier in the book, throughout the writings of early philosophers and theorists, there are countless references to the unmistakable mystic connection between the seven known planets of the time, and Earthly affairs, ailments and objects. Seven metals were connected with the seven planets, to which seven colours and the seven 'transformations' were added. So the ancient alchemist came to share the astrological doctrine that each planet ruled a mineral: The Sun ruled gold, the Moon silver, Mars iron, Venus copper, Saturn lead, Jupiter tin, and Mercury quicksilver. Consequently, in alchemical symbolism the same sign came to represent the nominated metal and its corresponding planet.

URANIUM

Aquarius's metal is uranium, a radioactive element that is used in research, as a fuel and perhaps as is best known, in nuclear weapons. Uranium owes its name to Uranus, the planet which was discovered a few years prior. The similarity between these two names, reminds us that scientific theory and thought can produce both brilliant and terrifying inventions.

Uranium is a very heavy metal which contains an abundant source of concentrated energy. Discovered in the eighteenth century, it is the principal fuel for nuclear reactors and the main raw material for nuclear weapons. It is no coincidence that the element associated with atomic energy is uranium, for the enormous power of the atom is equal to the power of Uranus. There are two ways to release this atomic power: through fission and through fusion. In fission, the heaviest atoms are split apart, and the resulting release of energy deposits radioactive waste which is extremely difficult to deal with, and potentially lethal to all life on our planet. In fusion, however, the lightest atoms are fused together, and the resulting release of energy does not pose a risk by leaving radioactive waste. Therefore, it makes sense that we can use this latter process to benefit mankind without the ominous possibility of destroying that which we are trying to improve. Uranus usually has the best of intentions, especially when it comes to serving humanity, so utilising it for the benefit of all, rather than the potential destruction of all, is undoubtedly far more desirable.

PLATINUM

The word 'platinum' originates from the Spanish word *plata*, meaning 'silver', referring to the colour of the metal. Platinum was discovered in the early 1700s. It is so rare that two million pounds of ore may only contain about one pound of platinum metal. Its rarity makes it even more valuable than gold. Platinum nuggets are rarely larger than a pea - anything larger would qualify as a major find. The highest quality platinum comes from the Ural Mountains in Russia. It can be used for jewellery, but has less glamorous uses too: it is placed in anti-pollution devices in cars to trap dirt and toxic gases.

LEAD

Lead is a chemical element in the carbon group with the symbol Pb (from Latin *plumbum*), and is a malleable, soft, corrosion-resistant, ductile and heavy metal which tarnishes to a dull greyish colour when exposed to air. When melted into a liquid, it has a shiny chrome lustre, and has been commonly used for thousands of years because it is widespread, easy to extract and easy to work with. Worldwide production and consumption of lead is increasing, with Australia, China and the United States accounting for more than half of primary production. However, with current usage rates, the supply of lead is estimated to run out in around forty years.

Contrary to popular belief, pencil leads in wooden pencils have never been made from lead, but rather a type of graphite called plumbago. Lead has many applications, including in the construction industry, batteries, pigments, the ballast keel of sailboats, cable sheathing, radiation protection, scuba diving weight belts, automobile parts and car batteries, electronic soldering, stained glass windows, organ pipes, gun bullets, ceramic glazes and plumbing.

Lead, however useful for many things, has its downside. If inhaled or swallowed, lead is a highly poisonous metal, affecting almost every organ, tissue and system in the body. The main target for lead toxicity is the nervous system, but it can also cause weakness in limbs and extremities, as well as rises in blood pressure. In pregnant women, high levels of exposure can cause miscarriage. Chronic, high-level exposure can also cause adverse brain and blood conditions, and has been linked to learning and other developmental disorders.

Lead is easy to work with, but it is toxic and therefore should not come into contact with bare skin. One way of using lead is to use parchment as a base and draw a circle around the symbols with a lead pin. Pewter can be and is often used as an alternative, because perhaps your power metal lead is best left to its more practical outer-world applications, well away from the body.

PLANTS, HERBS, SPICES, TREES, SHRUBS, FLOWERS, SCENTS & INCENSE

Plants have long been associated with magic, medicinal properties, superstition, nutrition and even astrology. In ancient times, some were endowed with magical properties based upon beliefs of the time, but also upon anecdotal evidence that some herbal concoctions, flowers or essences helped alleviate and even cure uncomfortable, painful or dis-eased physical or mental states. Whether these were based upon 'old wives' tales' or beliefs in supernatural forces matters little, for in modern times we can prove and indeed *have* proven through scientific research and controlled experiments, that plants have their place in our health and medicine cabinets. Some 'magical' plants have aphrodisiac or narcotic properties, while others have formidable toxic effects, but all are considered in some way to affect the human system on physical, spiritual and psychological levels. Plants such as cocoa, tobacco and coffee, which have accompanied humans over the course of millennia, are still, more than ever, an integral part of our daily lives. They still incite the same pleasures, the same fascinations, and the same dangers, and some still carry the same taboos. It is interesting to note that more than 80 per cent of chemical medicines in existence today, and found in pharmacists' dispensaries, are made from plants.

In modern astrology herbs are often associated with the zodiac signs and have evolved from an old system where a specific planet rules each herb. The planet that governs a herb is chosen according to its appearance, scent and where it grows; herbs are additionally categorised as hot or cold, and dry or moist. In this way you can see how the nature of the herb corresponds to the nature of the planet. If you are familiar with your ruling planets' basic associations, you will find it easy to match it to herbs. Although you can simply buy whatever herbs you wish to use for your magic, the optimum effect will be obtained if you can gather them at a favourable astrological time. Once you are armed with astrological knowledge, you can choose a time when the planet that rules your chosen herb is in a position of strength. Keep in mind that each planet rules a substantial amount of plants, so if one isn't easily obtained, it should be simply to find another one to use for the same purpose.

There sometimes seems to be a wide variance in the list of herbs associated with a specific astrological influence. This is because the different parts of the plant have different rulerships and uses. For example, whichever planet rules it, a plant that bears fruit is naturally related to Jupiter, its flowers relate to Venus, seed or bark to Mercury, leaves to the Moon, wood to Mars, and roots to Saturn. So, as well as the planet that traditionally rules the plant, it can be regarded as having a secondary ruler according to the part of the plant being used. Although you don't need to work with a highly complex system of deciding which herb will suit your purposes, you can make your magical workings more powerful by paying attention to some of these nuances.

Essentially, different scents, herbs, flowers and plants have their own specific vibrations. Their essences should be worn on your skin (you can make up your own combinations using essential oils or flower waters), burned in an oil burner, inhaled from a cloth, diffused in a bath or bowl of steam, or burned as incense sticks. Many plants, herbs and spices, however used, contain gentle yet effective energies which will affect not only your wishing ceremonies, but also your moods, associations and emotions, which can assist in carrying your wonderful Self in the direction of your dreams. Lifted up on incense smoke, for example, your wish is carried out to the wider Universe. Try making your own, out of any or all of your power plants, woods, flowers, shrubs, trees or herbs!

Thirty-three magical, mythical plants are: Cocoa, rosemary, tobacco, thyme, wheat, coffee, sugar cane, cinnamon, hemp, tea, pumpkin, foxglove, incense, amanita (a mushroom), tarragon, pepper, rice, belladonna, reed, ginseng, clove, ginger, sage, maize, mistletoe, lily, mandrake, St John's Wort, poppy, peyote, cinchona, verbena and the vine *. How many of your Aquarian 'lucky plants' (listed under the next sub-category, 'Your Lucky Plants, Herbs, Spices', etc.) can be found on this Magical 33 List?

YOUR LUCKY PLANTS, HERBS, SPICES, TREES, SHRUBS, FLOWERS, SCENTS, OILS & INCENSE

Gardenia, Azalea, Daffodil, Carnation, Violet, Pine, Ragwort, Cypress, Frankincense, Passionflower,

Barley, Snake Root, Skullcap, Olive, Marshmallow, Primula, Laurel, Prickly Ash, Celandine, Valerian, Lady's Slipper, Hops, Wood Sage, Myrrh, Rowan, All Heal, Ginger, Sorrel, Garlic, Apple, Apple Blossom, Orchid, Pear, Dancing Lady, Mandrake, Golden-Rain, Mint, Snowdrop, Chamomile, Catnip, Southernwood, Elderberry, Fuchsia, Foxglove, Verbena, Mountain Ash, most fruit trees. *

For Saturn ★ Aconite, Hemlock, Deadly Nightshade, Horsetail, Yew. Woody perennials also relate to Saturn. These include Chamomile, Linden Flowers, Thistle & Black Poppy Seeds *

* Some plant products can be poisonous, toxic, hallucinogenic or even fatal if consumed. Always research first.

YOUR SPECIAL POWER FLOWERS

AQUARIUS IN GENERAL ★ Orchid ★ A symbol of luxury, love and refinement.

OTHER BIRTH FLOWERS ★ Foxglove, Gentian & Snowdrop

JANUARY BORN ★ Carnation ★ To those born in January, the much-loved carnation promises a life of variety and empowers them with the quality of courage. Carnations remove negative energy, especially in close relationships, and in the Netherlands, red carnations are associated with love, energy and optimism. The carnation is an important flower in the Christian tradition, as it is believed carnations sprung up everywhere the Virgin Mary's tears fell as she walked to her son's crucifixion. In Mexico they are known as 'the flowers of the dead', as they are strewn around the bodies of the deceased as they are prepared for burial. Carnation can offer one protection and, depending on the colour, encouragement, love or admiration.

FEBRUARY BORN ★ Violet ★ As a birth flower, thanks to Christian symbolism, the violet symbolises the gentle qualities of modesty, humility and shyness (which is where the term *shrinking violet* comes from), together with strength of character in adversity. The Greeks associated the violet with Io, who was one of many human women loved by Zeus. Napoleon loved violets, and he used them to give hope to his followers. When he was exiled to Elba, he told his supporters that he would return, just as the violets return each spring, and as a result they used the violet as their symbol. Napoleon became affectionately known as "Caporal Violet" and gave a bunch to Josephine on their wedding day. On their anniversary each year he gave her another bunch of them, and after she died he placed a violet from her grave into a locket, and wore it around his neck until his own death.

YOUR FOODS

Aquarians love to experiment with new ideas, methods, foods, dishes and recipes - if indeed they follow recipes at all; most will invent their own concoctions as they go. If you're a truly typical Aquarian you'll adore eating out, and the more varied, eclectic and obscure the cuisine the better. You often enjoy the discovery of new tastes and textures more than the actual act of eating them. The person who samples Cambodian fried tarantulas, Vietnamese snake wine, Australian witchetty grubs, Indonesian luwak excrement, is likely to be born under the sign of Aquarius; the quirkier the dish, the more appealing it will be! Furthermore, you love to eat meals or unusual foods that can provide a fascinating conversation-starter for the next dinner party. Boring, bland or tedious is definitely not on the menu for the Water Bearer.

AQUARIUS POWER FOODS

"Let food be your medicine; let medicine be your food."
Hippocrates

Health Foods, Peppers, Barley, Celery, Apples, Figs, All Vegetables, Limes, Star Fruit, Chillies, Kiwi Fruits, Forest Berries, Dried Fruits, Kumquats, and any foods with sharp, distinctive or unusual flavours. Your power beverages are Vodka, Fumitory Tea, Mullern Tea, and Fad Health Drinks. *

* Caution: Always use essential oils, alcohol and/or herbs with caution and research each one prior to use, as not all are safe for use by certain people, or under certain conditions such as pregnancy, intoxication or illness. Some herbs and oils may be hallucinogenic, toxic in high doses, or produce other undesirable effects, and may be considered potentially harmful or hazardous if used or consumed before operating machinery, driving, or combined with alcohol or other drugs. Always consult a qualified practitioner or undertake thorough research from reliable sources before use or consumption of any of the listed essential oils, herbs or foods.

YOUR LUCKY WOOD ★ PINE
(Great to make a magic wand out of!)

Native Americans referred to trees as 'Standing People' because they stand firm, obtaining strength from their connection with the Earth. They therefore teach us the importance of being grounded, while at the same time listening to, and reaching towards, our higher aspirations. In Norse mythology, Yggdrasil, the tree of life, is a cosmic map that represents all life. The tree has its roots in the Underworld, is linked to the Earth through its trunk and its branches reach into the air of the Otherworld of spirit. The dryad, or tree's spirit, needs to be respected and asked when 'taking' from a tree for the purposes of magic. The essence of tree magic lies in understanding the qualities of each type. These can be drawn on for such things as healing and spell-casting. For example, the rowan tree grows high up the sides of mountains, often in hard-to-reach places, so if you need to develop tenacity or access to difficult spiritual spaces, you can call on this tree; the oak tree is durable and strong, so if you are needing fortification or firmness, you can gain power from this tree. When respected as living, breathing beings, trees can provide insights into the workings of Nature, cycles, and our own inner essence. Each birth time is associated with a particular kind of tree, the basic qualities of which complement the nature of those born during that time. Appreciate the beauty of your affinity tree and study its nature carefully, for it has a connection with your own nature and lessons to impart.

★ **PINE** ★ Pine wood corresponds to the elements of Fire and Air, and is purifying and cleansing to your physical environment, your personal 'space' and your overall person. In a magical sense, pine represents abundance, purification, creativity, healing, fertility and protection. It is excellent for attracting prosperity and to keep you 'on course' when your life or dreams seem to have deviated off their intended paths; its grace and stateliness serves as a reminder to always look upwards and to think positively. It also brings about inner peace, serenity, tranquillity, fertility, abundance, health, love and optimism. Excellent for use in rising above difficulties, pine is ultimately cleansing, uplifting, rejuvenating, purifying, and sanctifying.

The Native Americans looked deeply into the shapes and habits of all beings that inhabited the Earth to learn of the powers embodied in their various forms. The circular shape of the pine tree and its ability to reach a substantial age were believed to teach of the endless cyclical wheel of time and the wisdom derived from travelling around it. according to this native wisdom, pine needles, which are wrapped at their base in small packets, were said to be reminiscent of the strength and sustenance available to humans in their unity; and the gentle and pliable wood of the pine represents strength in its softness.

To the Chinese, pine was an emblem of immortality. They planted it on graves, for the green of its leaves, which were believed to be full of chi, the vital force, and could prevent the decay of the corpse while strengthening the spirit of the departed.

Branches of pine have been used in seasonal outdoor rituals, serving a role in purifying areas of outdoor worship by sweeping the forest floor before their performance.

Pine wood, cones, branches and needles all contain unique magical powers. Pine needles and boughs are especially good for bringing luck and prosperity, while pine cones are a potent symbol of fertility. Hanging pine in any form above the doorway or mantel of your house is believed to bring good fortune to those who dwell therein. The resin of pine can be burned to clear negative energies from the air, and the smoke is said to repel evil and send it back to its source.

Where pine trees have been given centuries of time and freedom to live and grow instead of being cut down by incessant human progress, their magical sentience is undeniably strong, their trunks standing solid and tall, their branches extending with the grace and complexity that grace and maturity can bring. Their enchanting eminence, coupled with their distinctive fragrance and magical properties, make pine a gentle but powerful force to work with.

YOUR SACRED CELTIC CALENDAR TREES
★ BIRCH OR ROWAN

BIRCH ★ (24 December - 20 January)
ROWAN (MOUNTAIN ASH) ★ (21 January - 17 February)

The Celts and other ancient peoples had many beliefs and traditions based around the magical lore of trees. The system of Celtic tree astrology was developed out of a natural connection with the Druids' knowledge of Earth cycles and their reverence for the sacred knowledge they believed was held by trees. The Druids had a profound connection with trees and regarded them as vessels of infinite wisdom. Their calendar, being based on a Lunar year of thirteen months, contains a tree for each of these Lunar months, corresponding with (but not exactly) each of the twelve western astrology zodiac signs, which are based on the Solar calendar. Because there are some crossovers, I have included two possible trees for your zodiacal birth period.

★ **BIRCH** ★ The word birch comes from the Sanskrit root *bharg^*, which means 'shining', for the areas in which it grows contain snow which melts and sends cascades of water down its trunk, the birch bark taking on an appearance of liquid glitter. When it rains, the bark becomes so wet and dark, it is named the black birch. Birch carries properties of protection, exorcism, healing and purification.

The medicine of the cherry birch lies in its inner bark, which contains a rich, fragrant oil known commercially as wintergreen. The name wintergreen hints at the birch's effectiveness as a transitional plant between winter and spring. Spiritually, the black birch assists us in locating within our own bodies the signs of spring which have been buried under winter's cold, barren landscape and its oil assists us in shedding our protective winter layer to make way for our fresh 'green' selves to sprout.

The cherry birch thrives when it grows near water, giving us a signature of its gift as a tonic to the Watery elements and needs of the human body. In Russian tradition, birch trees were deeply revered through song and story. But while eastern European folklore focuses on the protective powers of birches, the Nordic countries consider birch the symbol of the Earth Mother, embodying the female, cyclical powers of growth and healing. Traditionally, witches' brooms are made of birch twigs, twine and wood, so if you feel drawn to witchcraft and the feminine aspects of magic and spirit, then birch wood might be a wise choice for you.

The immense durability of birch bark has been put to many uses; from Native American canoes and ropes to writing parchment. Using birch bark as a medium for the written word strengthens your connection to the tree's claim of being a 'tree of knowledge' and a gateway to new ideas and worlds. The tough substance of this bark indeed survives long after the original tree has died. Although strong, it is easy to work with.

In western Europe, the beautiful and graceful birch is referred to as the 'Lady of the Woods', belonging to the element of Water and under the dominion of the planet Venus. It is believed that if one wishes to communicate with the goddess, one should sit silently in a grove of birches and listen for her whispers, which travel on the gentle wisps of wind.

Throughout its life cycle, the birch continues to be both a useful and versatile resource. As a pioneer tree, it gives way to other larger trees, sacrificing itself to make way for new life. It is therefore associated with the circle of life, endings and beginnings, and new growth.

The birch tree is the Celtic tree of beginnings, an association springing from the fact that it is the first tree to grow back after a forest fire. The birch also sheds its bark, which suggests further links with renewal, as the old and worn-out is released to make way for the new. Creating and carrying a staff or wand made out of white birch wood is an ancient, wise way of allying one's self with qualities of communication, truth, perception and clearer vision. Wands can be fashioned and used to point the way to clear intent and fresh beginnings in life, or a kind of rebirthing of the soul.

The silver birch tree has special associations with the Moon as, interestingly, its bark reflects the moonlight, making the tree appear to glow in the light of a Full Moon.

★ **ROWAN** ★ Rowan is the magical tree of protection, healing and success. Due to the conditions in which it grows, the rowan tree symbolises tenacity. It is found growing high up on the sides of mountains, often sprouting from tiny crevices in inaccessible spots. The rowan tree is chiefly grown for its beauty, its seasonally rich red berries adding to its appeal.

Ruled by the Celtic fire goddess Brigid, the rowan is believed to be endowed with powerful magic and healing properties. In mythology, the rowan is sacred to Brigid, or Bride, who is often depicted carrying a flaming torch of inspiration, and who is remembered in the first fire festival of the Celtic calendar, Imbolc. During this celebration, the druids would build towers of rowan and lie within them, entering into a meditative trance-like state. These rituals added to the tree's reputation for bestowing prophecy and spiritual insight.

Rowan berries bear the magical pentagram - an important symbol in magical traditions. The rowan berry has a tiny five-pointed star or pentagram opposite its stalk, which earned the tree its other title of 'Witch Tree'. It is thought that the rowan is a tree of enchantment, containing wood that can be used for Otherworldly magic. The druids burned its wood before a battle, in order to contact the fairies in the Otherworld to ask for their aid. This protective property perhaps also explains why it was worn, hung in doorways, or planted near houses to offer protection against evil forces.

ESPECIALLY FOR AUSTRALIANS
(OF ALL ZODIAC SIGNS)

If you live in Australia, here are two Australian-based magical woods, for those who prefer to source their woods closer to home and nature. Australia has a less documented history than many European civilisations, but still has no less mythology and legends swirling in its mists of time.

EUCALYPTUS ★ Eucalyptus is very plentiful and has a wonderfully intoxicating, distinctive, clean aroma which is reminiscent of the continent's vast areas of bushland, and has played an important ceremonial and medicinal role in the culture of Australian Aborigines, who have inhabited the nation for 40,000 to 50,000 years. Eucalyptus is a wood of feminine energy whose elemental association is Earth and main origin is Australia. One of the strongest healing woods known, eucalyptus wood has been used for centuries for medicinal as well as ritualistic purposes. Heady and Earthy, the energy of this wood is clean and pure. Eucalyptus is recommended for the promotion of good, robust health, and is also related to luck, especially if regarding knowledge. An excellent tool in divination, particularly when worn as a charm to invoke luck, it brings the wearer or user good fortune when used in rituals seeking positive results.

LEOPARDWOOD (or LACEWOOD) ★
Leopardwood or the Leopard Tree, so named because of its spotted wood, carries the energies of both the masculine and the feminine, Mars (Aries, Scorpio) and Venus (Taurus, Libra), and its main affinity is with the Water element (Cancer, Scorpio, Pisces). Leopardwood is a very useful tool for divination and is associated with positive luck, earning it the label 'gambler's wood'. Overall, its energy is very positive, making it an ideal wood for use in almost any ritual or spell, especially those concerning luck, magic and divination.

THE POWER OF LOVE

Each Sun sign exudes their own love and romance style. This style is an energy unique to that sign, and has the power to magnetise to that person their true, soulful match. Unhappy or unsuccessful relationships are often the result of incompatible Sun signs, personal values, goals, hopes, viewpoints or expectations. I believe everyone has a perfect soul partner (or three!) who is especially for them, and just knowing that special person or persons are out there can illuminate your life's romantic path. In this lifetime, we may not find that person or persons, but can still experience the joys and wonders of many other significant relationships which enrich and add tremendous meaning to our lives. Some partnerships are only fleeting, but the feelings they give us can last a lifetime, while others are more enduring, and the rewards they give us and lessons they teach us can last a lifetime too. Small gestures of love on a frequent basis, consistent nurturing and communication, and making the effort to understand each other, are just four ways to keep the fires of passion and romance burning long after the initially roaring fire has diminished into glowing embers.

Your whole natal chart would need to be examined to form an overall picture of your romantic nature, and although the Sun is a fantastic starting point, it is not the sole consideration. Regarding these other planets, in Carl Jung's studies on psychological astrology, and in traditional synastry (the comparing of two people's natal charts to determine overall compatibility), the harmonious link between the Sun in one person's chart and the Moon in the other's (usually the man's Sun and the woman's Moon) is considered the best indication for a happy and enduring relationship. More specifically, the sextile aspect, an angle of 60 degrees, appeared most frequently between the Sun of one and the Moon of the other in fulfilling relationships. Other positive planetary contacts, such as one person's Moon to another's Venus, or the Mars to the Moon (again, traditional indications of attraction and harmony) also occurred frequently.

The feminine personal planets in a male's chart (Moon and Venus), and the masculine personal planets in a female's chart (Sun and Mars) tell a lot about the inner self and how this is projected onto relationships. However helpful chart analysis is in telling a story about your relationship style and approach, it all depends not on your chart, but on what you do with the resources at your disposal, which your chart can indeed tell you a lot about. Relationships and marriages involving harmonious planetary and zodiacal energies between the two people tend to last longer because they are simply more 'flowing' and easier.

The signs in which the four personal and 'relationship' planets - the Sun, the Moon, Venus and Mars - are placed, coupled with the aspects they make with the other planets in the chart, give important clues into understanding the often unconscious drives within you that shape your relating style, tastes, mannerisms and patterns.

Expanding upon the other planetary considerations is beyond the scope of this book, but it is useful to know, particularly if you are interested in examining the dynamics of a current relationship a bit deeper, or are wishing to attract a new one into your life. But for now, your Sun sign is a wonderful place to start! Your Solar sign is regarded as being at the core of the complex - and very fun - study of relationships! So for now, we will begin this study of love with your essence, your core self, the brightest light shining from within - your Sun sign!

SOME LUCKY-IN-LOVE TIPS
GENERAL HINTS

★ To attract and retain love, the Heart chakra (an energy centre within the body) needs to be balanced and clear from blockages. The Heart chakra is located in the region of the physical heart. Its Sanskrit name is *anahata*, and its symbol is a twelve-petal green lotus flower whose centre contains a green circle and two intersecting triangles making up a six-pointed star representing balance (and also could be said to symbolise six as the number of Venus). Its element is Air and its colour is green. Balance in this chakra is expressed as unconditional love for ourselves and others. Crystals that can be used to cleanse and balance this chakra are mostly green and pink stones.

★ Pink candles (two, representing a couple, or six, representing Venus, is preferable) can be used in love spells.

★ Any 'love-attracting' wishing rituals should be done on a Friday (ruled by Venus) night around the time of the New Moon (signifying the principle of increase and growth).

★ Basil, otherwise known as witch's herb or St Joseph's wort, is said to be the most potent lover herb of all. Basil vibrates to the energy of Mars, which is all about lust and sexual energy, and it is used prolifically in all sorts of love potions and rituals throughout the world.

★ Ginger has a reputation as a potent sexual tonic and aphrodisiac *. Arousing and warm, it can increase sensual vitality, particularly in men. Being warming and spicy, its vibration aligns with Mars. Saffron is also regarded as a potent, albeit expensive, aphrodisiac!

★ Wear red and pink (associated with Mars and Venus respectively), as these colours in all their shades are said to incite passion, lust and romance. Green is also connected with the heart by virtue of its association with the Heart chakra and the planet Venus, and its links with fertility, nature, abundance of all kinds, and new growth.

★ Call upon some higher spiritual help. When working your 'love magic', some planetary influences, goddesses and gods that you can call upon are: Aphrodite, Venus and Eros/Cupid, and other lesser known deities such as Juno Lucina, Demeter, Freya, Ishtar, Circe and Hathor.

★ The planet Venus has developed a rich culture of gods and goddesses associated with her varying levels of love and passion. These include the virgin - Brighid; the fertile woman - Aphrodite, (the Greek goddess); and of course Venus (the Roman equivalent); the mother and provider - Demeter; and desirous or physical love - Eros/Cupid (Venus's son).

★ The pine tree is sacred to Adonis (Venus's lover) and is said to balance the male and female energies. Pine is cleansing and protective and, as an evergreen, symbolises life. Its cones represent fertility.

★ Cardamom is said to have aphrodisiac qualities

★ The three almost universally recognised symbols of love are the goddesses Venus and Aphrodite, and the Cupid. Venus is the patroness of flowers and vegetation, and represents the regenerative cycle of creation, as well as beauty, herbs and physical love. She can be called upon for general love wishes and rituals. The dove, roses, rings, copper, apples, rosemary and the ankh are some of her sacred symbols. Aphrodite is a Greek goddess who has the ability to brings lovers together. Her names mean 'of the sea' as she is believed to have been born of the foam of the ocean. She can be called upon in ceremonies and spells for affection, love, marriage and partnership. Some of her associated symbols are the Flower of Aphrodite, swans, dolphins, frankincense and myrrh. Cupid, the cherubic winged boy with a bow and arrow, is the Roman name, and Eros is the Greek name for the same deity. The son of Venus/Aphrodite, he is an aspect that represents lustful love and desire.

★ Heartsease, another name for the wild pansy, Latin viola tricolour, was one of the most popular additives to the love potions of the ancient Romans and Greeks.

★ In centuries past, when people were more in tune with nature and its cycles, ceremonies, rituals and festivals were held on certain dates or times of year. The following are some examples, and you can reawaken their powers through craft and ceremony: February 2 is Bridhid's Day, or Bride's Day, and represents the white goddess; February 14 is Valentine's Day, traditionally the greatest and most well-known love 'celebration' of the year; March 1 is one of the festival days of Juno Lucina, the light bearer and goddess of women and marriage; the month of April is especially linked to the love goddess Aphrodite; the Summer solstice which falls on or around June 21 is an important time for reconnecting with the spirit of love, fertility and marriage; August 1 is the first of three harvest festivals in the Celtic calendar: The Harvest Festival honours Demeter, the goddess of love, as bountiful mother and faithful wife; the Festival of Lights, Diwali, in October, is sacred to Lakshmi, the Hindu goddess of happiness, love, and good fortune; the Winter solstice which falls on or around December 21, marks the turning point from long dark nights to lengthening days, and is the time of the wheel of love when virgin goddesses gave birth to their children - it is also fittingly symbolised by evergreens such as pine, ivy and holly; in Mexico, December 31, the last night of the year, is traditionally 'wishing night' and is an opportune time to make a wish for a lover in the coming year, using evergreen branches to enhance your request.

* The term 'aphrodisiac' is derived from Aphrodite, the Greek goddess of love, beauty, lust and sensuality

★ GEMSTONES ★

When it comes to calling love into your life using crystals, the general rule is that any of the pink or green stones are closely aligned with matters of the heart and can therefore help you to entice the affections you seek. Although your Sun sign has its very own special gemstones, outlined elsewhere in the book, the following stones can be used by all the signs (except for the first point, which are your own sign's feature stones), as their energies and qualities contain the power to attract and create love in all its forms, from self-love to deeper soulful connections with another, or to increase states of being which open the heart, thus enhancing your abilities to magnetise love.

★ Amethyst, Garnet and Aquamarine ★ Using your Aquarian luckiest crystals is a fabulous start to working on heightening your romantic zest, and making your sensual energy more potent. Zircon, Jacinth and Jargoon are also useful in raising your attracting powers.

★ Rose Quartz is the ultimate love stone. It invites love into your life by helping to open your heart to receive love, and gently reminding you that you are worthy of love. Connected with the Heart chakra, it is the stone of unconditional love, enhancing all forms of it and opening up the heart. It is excellent for increasing self-worth and acceptance. The colour of rose quartz is pink, the colour of Venus, the amorous planet of desire and nurturance. Balancing and calming, it helps to heal emotional pain. Wear this stone, keep some beside your bed, or sleep with some under your pillow to remind you that love it coming your way - and that you whole*heart*edly deserve it!

★ Green Aventurine is considered the 'opportunity and luck stone'. Connected with the Heart chakra, it helps us to recognise opportunities and is said to place us exactly where we need to be for good things to transpire, as energetically it opens our mind and heart to increased perception to recognise lucky elements. It also promotes new growth, optimism, and is an overall attractor of good fortune, adventure and abundance.

★ Jade, on a spiritual level, has an affinity with the Heart chakra. It harmonises relationships, and encourages compassion and the establishment of strong bonds.

★ Emerald is reputedly a stone of constancy in love, and is said to have been brought to Earth from the planet Venus. Because it is green, it also holds deep associations with the Heart chakra.

★ Rhodochrosite can be used to attract one's soul mate. This stone, as with all the pink stones, can be used as an effective love magnet. It encourages you to appreciate yourself by teaching you that you are worthy of love, wholeness and happiness - and so opening you up to receive.

★ Malachite, Citrine, Rhodonite, Moonstone, Morganite, Beryl, Ruby, Mangano Calcite, Garnet, Red and Pink Tourmaline, Tugtupite, Rutilated Quartz, Lodestone, Peridot and Lapis Lazuli are also known for their love properties, and can be used or worn to invite romance into your life, or to bring and retain enduring love.

★ Clear Quartz can be used with any of these listed crystals to amplify their metaphysical properties.

★ Shells: Although shells are not technically a crystal, but rather a natural elemental material, they are associated with love and are sacred to Aphrodite, the Greek love goddess, and are often used in magic talismans to attract romance.

★ ESSENTIAL OILS ★

The following essential oils are known for their aphrodisiac or love-attracting properties also, and can be worn as perfumes on the skin, used in an oil burner or vaporiser, dispersed in a bath, used in spell-casting and wishing rituals, sprinkled on your pillow to imbue your dreams with inspired romantic notions, or in any other creative ways you can think of! **

★ Essential oils, flowers and herbs which contain natural pheromones or like substances, or increase pheromone levels in the body, are: Lavender, Frankincense, Jasmine, Nutmeg, Ylang Ylang, Sandalwood, Patchouli and Asian Agarwood (Oud).

★ The prime love oil, which holds universal appeal, is rose. Reputedly excellent for both the mind and body, roses are the basis of more than 95 per cent of women's fragrances, and the petals have a long tradition of uplifting the spirits and soothing the soul. *Rosa damascena* is believed to be good for attracting love, while *R. centifolia*, the French rose oil base, is regarded as an aphrodisiac. Rose is traditionally accepted as the all-encompassing universal fragrance of love, blessed with a reputation for opening up the hearts of all those who come under its spell.

★ Cedarwood oil has been used since ancient times in incense and perfumes. Its deep, woody scent helps to stimulate the Base chakra, increasing sexual passion and desire. Its sedative qualities aid relaxation and encourage openness. In herbal magic, it is also associated with spells for wealth and abundance.

★ Neroli, Geranium, Almond (as a base), Basil, Thyme, Vetiver, Gardenia, Vanilla, Rose Otto, Apple, Cardamom, Lotus, Orange, Ginger, Bergamot, Rosewood and Clary Sage are also exquisitely seductive and sensual, and can be used in any way you like to bring to you that which your heart desires. These oils, when mixed with your own pheromones and magical intentions, will naturally enhance your point of attraction!

** Always research first and use with caution.

AQUARIUS ★ LOVE STYLE

A union with Aquarius will be different from traditional relationships. This has the advantage that boredom and routine are excluded to a large degree, but also the disadvantage that your long-suffering partner may never know what's quite going on. Anyone who falls in love with you should be prepared for everything and anything, except a steady, predictable life. Therefore, the lover of an Aquarius needs to be extremely flexible and tolerant of your many whims and fanciful ideals. Living in a world of ideas rather than emotions, you tend to repress your feelings. Charmingly naïve in most romantic adventures, you are often sincere to the extent that you don't know when someone is attracted to you, and you are incapable of play the Don Juan role unless you really mean it. Romantic escapades are not your style, for you are often unsure of yourself and awkward. However, you are a truly interesting companion and utterly intriguing lover, keeping your partner on his or her toes at all times. To Uranian-ruled Aquarius, love is generally open and friendly, but you may come across glamorously aloof. As a lover and in relationships, you are afraid of deep emotional involvement and may find it difficult to sustain close relationships, because this means adjusting your lifestyle to accommodate the habits of another, but are extremely loyal and faithful once committed. Love and friendship is sacred to you and you will delight your partners with surprises or lashings of help or advice, but you also have the tendency to suddenly disappear from circulation and immerse yourself in a project. As a lover you are cool and detached, unpredictable and zany, but you can also defrost without warning and be very passionate.

Odd is normal to you so you might thrill your lover with quirky gifts, then forget the 'normal' things like birthday presents and anniversary dates. You value friendship above all else, and in any close relationship you tend to guard your independence and freedom, and often enjoy unconventional or even living-apart relationships. Any heavy emotional demands, possessive behaviour, dramatic scenes, or overt expressions of sentimentality have you packing your bags and climbing out the window in no time. You like your partner to share or even take over the chores of the home, as housework hinders your much-valued liberty. Moreover, you expect your lover to allow your personal freedom of movement and action, have a respect for your many friends, and have an understanding and tolerance of your oddities, and in return you offer unwavering loyalty, genuine companionship and faithfulness. If your relationship is based on friendship, it is more likely to endure than one that isn't. For you after all, lust, passion and sex need a solid base.

LUCKY IN LOVE? AQUARIUS ★ COMPATIBILITY

* Please note the following is based on your Sun sign alone. For a whole and integrated approach to relationship compatibility, your whole natal chart would need to be taken into consideration. Synastry (*syn*: acting or considered together, united; *astry*: pertaining to the stars) is a branch of astrology which delves into more complex areas, and is based upon the natal charts of the two people concerned, to determine overall compatibility, potential conflicts and suitability based upon celestial influences. For the purposes of length, the below information is simplified and only refers to Sun sign connections.

Aquarius ★ Aries ♒ ♈

The interaction between your ruling planets, Mars and Uranus, and your elements, Air and Fire, ensures there will indeed be tremendous power between you two. Aquarius will never hamper Aries's independence or initiative, and Aries is likely to feel inspired by Aquarius's lively and friendly company. Aries loves anything novel, so Aquarius' offbeat character will appeal, but the hot-headed and passionate Ram is likely to become impatient and irritated with the Water Bearer's unpredictability, cool indifference and aloofness at times. When ideas flow, you are at your best together. Despite the mental affinity, that Aquarian coolness can confuse and concern Aries. Aries will also not always readily tolerate the 'embrace-all-peace-love-and-brotherhood' attitude of Aquarius, as Aries likes to always be right in the centre of the (relationship's) Universe. If used constructively, however, this is a wonderful match which will fulfil, uplift and inspire both signs.

Overall compatibility rating ★ 8 out of 10
Lucky Romance Tip ★ To attract an Aries, wear the colours red or orange, and use the crystal diamond

Aquarius ★ Taurus ♒ ♉

Aquarians can make you see red - with either passion or anger! Either way, they easily slip out of your grasp and fly off into the world of ideas and freedom - and at the most unexpected times! Very different in nature, you have little in common except your more negative expressions, such as stubbornness, unwillingness to change and inflexibility. Taurus is possessive while Aquarius values freedom; Taurus is affectionate while Aquarius is generally cool; Taurus is simple while Aquarius embraces complexities; Taurus is sensual and seeks security while Aquarius is experimental and seeks novel experiences; Taurus is traditional while Aquarius challenges the establishment; Taurus is domestic while Aquarius loathes being chained to the kitchen sink; Taurus deals with tangible and practical realities while Aquarius is idealistic and dwells in the abstract and unusual. Both share the Fixed mode, meaning there is a certain obstinacy and potential for frequent locking of horns that may hinder their progress. Taurus finds it difficult to understand Aquarius's unconventional and unpredictable nature, while Aquarians spread themselves far and wide socially, finding it difficult to fulfil Taurus's need for exclusivity in a relationship.

Overall compatibility rating ★ 5 out of 10
Lucky Romance Tip ★ To attract a Taurus, wear the colours pink or green, and use the crystal rose quartz

Aquarius ★ Gemini ♒ ♊

Aquarian eccentricity will amuse and enchant the Twins, and they will be attracted to the sociable side of the Aquarian personality. But Aquarius, being a fixed sign, takes loyalty very seriously, and may not appreciate Gemini's flirtatious bent. You can delight each other with your mental gymnastics and this can be a fine friendship and a sparkling romance. Gemini's easy going charm will fascinate the more serious Aquarian. Both thinking and mentally-oriented Air signs, you have the potential to make beautiful music together. Gemini can usually accept Aquarius's erratic and detached moods, and both will give each other the space they need in the relationship. Gemini is stimulated by Aquarius's dazzling intellect and Aquarius in turn is inspired by Gemini's lively mind. The headstrong, wilful, stubborn characteristics of the Water Bearer may be trying for the Twins' fickle, Mutable, flexible nature, and Gemini's restlessness may make Aquarius dizzy at times. Similarly, Aquarius's rebelliousness may frazzle and fray the much less complex Twins' nerves. But one thing is certain: The Water Bearer will always keep Gemini on his agile toes and wits! These two can usually work through most differences, however, and there will never be a dull moment, especially in the social arena, in which you both spend most of your time. The unconventional and changeable quality of this relationship helps to keep it interesting, and neither is likely to smother the other, but you both may be so busy mingling in your many separate activities and friendship circles that you forget to make time for each other!

Overall compatibility rating ★ 9 out of 10
Lucky Romance Tip ★ To attract a Gemini, wear the colours light blue or yellow, and use the crystal citrine

Aquarius ★ Cancer ♒ ♋

Your ruling planets, the Moon and Uranus, will exercise two very different energies in your relationship. Further, your elements Air and Water, and your modes Fixed and Cardinal, don't blend easily. The Crab will prove too emotional and clingy for the intellectually-inclined, freedom-seeking Aquarius, and Cancer will find Aquarius's naturally cool and aloof nature unsettling, and perhaps even hurtful to their highly sensitive nature. Cancer is private while Aquarius loves to share; Cancer is personal while Aquarius is impersonal; Cancer is home-loving while Aquarius feels stifled when domestically 'caged in'; Cancer seeks sentimental love and a meeting of the hearts, while Aquarius seeks friendship and a meeting of the minds. Overall, Aquarius is a Universal rather than a personal lover, who likes to share interests and ideas with friends and humanity, and Cancer has a protective, security-seeking nature whose interests lie primarily in her home, children and family life.

Overall compatibility rating ★ 5 out of 10
Lucky Romance Tip ★ To attract a Cancerian, wear the colours silver or white, and use the crystal moonstone

Aquarius ★ Leo ♒ ♌

While you two are astrological opposites, you are not necessarily psychological opposites, as your elements, Air and Fire, blend well together. In fact, being cosmic opposites, you have much to teach each other, and each can learn invaluable relationship lessons from the other. Both being Fixed signs, you also share strong minds, fixed opinions, a strong determination and each a mind of your own. These qualities can be used constructively to form a wonderful bond between you, but there will inevitably be clashes of wills, especially if the Water Bearer takes flight, as they are prone to do from time to time, and the Lion doesn't get his way. The Lion appreciates the Water Bearer's quirky sense of humour, but the Aquarian's cool demeanour can dampen the romance somewhat. Leo will not understand why Aquarius should be so unpredictable, detached and unreachable at the most unexpected times and for no apparent reason. Leo needs adoration, praise and to be the centre of attention, and will not always appreciate Aquarius's need for sharing and caring on a wider scale. Leo's pride can be easily wounded by Aquarius's independence and lack of consistent affection, and although you both enjoy varied company, the Water Bearer is more detached and impersonal in social groups. Overall, if used positively, Leo and Aquarius can share a joyful and stimulating relationship, if they can overcome their differences. Indeed, Air will usually fuel the Fire here, making it burn bigger and brighter.

Overall compatibility rating ★ 7.5 out of 10
Lucky Romance Tip ★ To attract a Leo, wear the colours gold or orange, and use the crystal ruby

Aquarius ★ Virgo ♒ ♍

Air and Earth generally don't blend well together, and although your ruling planets, Uranus and Mercury, are similar in nature, this only emphasises a mental and intellectual affinity between your very different signs, rather than a deep emotional bond. The Water Bearer is a difficult yet fascinating creature to the Virgin. The Aquarian's quick inventive flow of ideas will enchant Virgo - until Virgo realises the Water Bearer has left the essential 'nuts and bolts' out of the scheme. The Aquarius's idealistic and unpredictable nature may also irritate Virgo's fragile nerves and make the Virgin more edgy than she already is. Virgo's nit picking and fussiness will get on Aquarius's nerves, and Aquarius's unpredictable, temperamental and unconventional nature will unsettle the orderly, rational and sensible Virgo. The Water Bearer's dispassionate and detached character may resonate somewhat with the Virgin's naturally cool and essentially unemotional psyche, but Virgo's natural tendency to anxiety and worrying will irk the more broad-minded Aquarius. Virgo can't see the forest for the trees, while the Water Bearer can see the entire forest *and* the trees. Overall, Virgo's need for logic and order are the furthest things from the erratic Aquarius's mind, and Virgo's natural, almost obsessive, tendencies towards cleanliness and tidiness are not concerns at all for the free-spirited, vague Aquarius, who has ever wider - and indeed Universal - concerns.

Overall compatibility rating ★ 5 out of 10
Lucky Romance Tip ★ To attract a Virgo, wear the colours white or yellow, and use the crystal sapphire

Aquarius ★ Libra ♒ ♎

As two Air signs together, you can be warm playmates or emotional tornadoes. The sceptic hidden beneath the Libran good cheer often doubts those lofty Aquarian ideals. But Air harmonises with Air, and these two also have the potential to have an intense and explosive meeting of the minds. Since these two signs are naturally friendly and need the company of others, they can share these pleasures together. However, Libra is the epitome of the personal lover, while Aquarius is the archetypal Universal lover who prefers to share interests and affections with many people. Libra's emphasis on close intimate relationships can also cause tension, as Aquarius needs to feel free and unencumbered by emotional ties. While Aquarius is largely aloof, eccentric and unpredictable, Libra uses diplomacy, grace and tact to handle things. Neither will make impossible demands on the other, as both are intellectually-based rather than feeling, smothering types, but this relationship can only work if Libra allows Aquarius freedom and does not demand too much 'together' time. Their intellectual rapport alone, however, suggests deep potential here, and can take their relationship to great heights.

Overall compatibility rating ★ 8.5 out of 10
Lucky Romance Tip ★ To attract a Libran, wear the colours pink and blue, and use the crystal opal

Aquarius ★ Scorpio ♒ ♏

A wild and difficult combination, yet the energy can also be enjoyable. If you can overcome your differences of style and take it slowly, yours can be an intoxicating match. But generally speaking, Air and Water don't tend to blend easily, and this is highlighted in this coupling. Scorpio is intensely emotional and naturally possessive, and this doesn't always sit too well with the freedom-loving, detached and unemotional Aquarius. Scorpio will feel rejected and left cold by Aquarius's apparent disregard for their complex feelings. If Scorpio tries to dominate the indomitable Aquarius, rebellion will result, and when a serious rift develops in this relationship, Aquarius can easily separate and cut the losses, while Scorpio may brood, sulk and harbour feelings of revenge or vindictiveness. Scorpio is passionate and controlling, while Aquarius is dispassionate and needs space. While the Water Bearer sees love in broader, Universal terms, the Scorpion views love in powerfully personal terms. Unless this significant difference in emotions is understood, Scorpio will feel that Aquarius is too indifferent and impersonal. Also, Aquarius's erratic nature will challenge Scorpio's all-or-nothing, extreme attitudes to life and love. Although there are many differences between you, being Fixed signs, you are both strong-willed and determined, so if you can channel your combined forces into a common goal, great achievements are possible in your partnership.

Overall compatibility rating ★ 6.5 out of 10
Lucky Romance Tip ★ To attract a Scorpio, wear the colours red or burgundy, and use the crystal malachite

Aquarius ★ Sagittarius ♒ ♏

Air and Fire have a strong affinity, as do your ruling planets Uranus, the lord of lightning, and Jupiter, the god of thunder. Water Bearers like to speak their minds and express their opinions as much as the Archer does, and you are both idealistic and overall very well-matched. As you both value idealism and freedom, this could make for an unpredictable, zany and unforgettable ride! These two will have a wonderful chemistry between them and make a strong impact on each other, but when the need arises, they both give each other the freedom they so desire. Both being independent and intellectual rather than deeply feeling, you share incredibly idealistic natures that usually remain as pie-in-the-sky notions, but which thrill you nonetheless, and can provide endless fodder for stimulating conversation. Indeed, you both love to share your sparkling ideals which transcend the personal, mundane level. The Archer has an uncanny ability to bring out the passionate side of the Water Bearer, and you are the most likely of all the combinations to be sexually compatible. Sagittarius's warm wit and charm will win over Aquarius's cool nature, and Aquarius's aloof glamour will appeal to the Sagittarian's accepting and embracing heart. You are both naturally friendly and gregarious, so are likely to attract and enjoy many resulting social pleasures and events together. Aquarius's eccentricities, quirks and unpredictability may perplex the more open-hearted Sagittarius, but will nonetheless provide an endless source of intrigue, delight and bedazzlement.

Overall compatibility rating ★ 9 out of 10
Lucky Romance Tip ★ To attract a Sagittarius, wear the colour deep purple or royal blue, and use the crystal zircon

Aquarius ★ Capricorn ♒ ♑

Capricorn supports the status quo and Aquarius likes to shake it up. The Goat should either loosen up and respect the Water Bearer's often kooky ideals, or choose another mountain to climb. While Aquarius, an Air sign, is erratic, unusual, disobedient, inventive, unorthodox and more than a little wayward,

Capricorn, an Earth sign, is traditional, sensible, practical, conventional and structured. Air and Earth do not mix very harmoniously, and your modes, Fixed and Cardinal, will also prove an obstacle to you two seeing eye to eye. Capricorn is tight, sometimes mean, and tenacious, striving for goals and lofty ambitions, while Aquarius is unpredictable but ever-friendly, and independent, determined to reach their ideals in a completely different way. Aquarian behaviour often undermines Capricorn's desire for stability, security and consistency. The rebellious Water Bearer likes to rock the boat, challenge the establishment, question authority, seek out thrills and break down outworn traditions, while the Goat is rigid, conservative and respectful of tradition and authority. You do share minds of a high order however, and if you can channel your energies into your intellectual rapport and natural respect for each other, a mutually fulfilling relationship could very well develop. Overall, Aquarius's capriciousness and unruly streak will unnerve and shock the quiet, steady Goat, who just wants to live a peaceful - albeit constantly achieving - life. Only time - of which Capricorn has an abundance - will tell with this pairing.

Overall compatibility rating ★ 6 out of 10
Lucky Romance Tip ★ To attract a Capricorn, wear the colours brown or black, and use the crystal garnet

Aquarius ★ Aquarius ♒ ♒

On the surface, both of you, sharing the same Sun and the same ruling planet, appear to be the picture of excitement, thrills and oddball adventures. However, too much Air may create two people who seem to get along like, well, a hurricane. Outsiders may not be able to fathom this complex Aquarian wavelength because it takes one to know another, and only these two can truly know why the other thinks or behaves as they do. You are both intellectual, independent, freedom-loving and detached, so there is a deep resonance and unspoken understanding at work here. Your ruling planet Uranus, may prove too much of a force and while initially providing fireworks and 'electricity', this energy can just as readily burn you both - or at least give your relationship an unpleasant electric jolt when you least expect it. Much will depend on the many facets of this sign each person reflects, but sooner or later, unusual, surprising or disruptive influences may affect your relationship. It does, however have the potential to be a strong bond, formed through the meeting of two incredibly intuitive, original and brilliant minds - just don't spend too much time apart by working in separate laboratories, or climbing different rainbows.

Overall compatibility rating ★ 8 out of 10
Lucky Romance Tip ★ To attract an Aquarian, wear the colours electric blue or turquoise, and use the crystal aquamarine

Aquarius ★ Pisces ♒ ♓

This is a surprisingly magical mix. Indeed, it would be hard to find a more unusual - and enlightening - combination than these two, for the simple reason that your ruling planets, Uranus and Neptune, are quite literally out of this world. Both signs have an elusive quality about them, and have a level of understanding that seems to contradict the usual Air/Water relating difficulties. You are both unique and different to most other people, and you sometimes feel like misfits, that is except around each other. Although the Piscean psyche is deep, emotional and complex, the Aquarian can still manage to sense the unfathomable depths of the Piscean soul. Feeling, sensitive and romantic, the Pisces seems to intuitively respect Aquarius's need for independence, freedom and friendships outside the relationship. You are both compassionate, caring, kind, humanitarian and believe in all things other-worldly and mystical, and although you express these in different ways, you can still find a way to live together in relative harmony with little effort. Perhaps this is because you are both lovers of solitude, for different reasons of course, but you understand each other's occasional need for retreat. If you can forget your elementary and modal (Fixed and Mutable) differences, you may just make a beautiful symphony together - indeed, you can swim along happily through life's meandering waters together, as long as Pisces doesn't try to escape or get lost along the way.

Overall compatibility rating ★ 7.5 out of 10

Lucky Romance Tip ★ To attract a Pisces, wear the colours mauve or sea green, and use the crystal amethyst

YOUR TAROT CARDS ★ FOR LUCK, MAGIC, ENERGY, ABUNDANCE, QUESTING & MEANING
THE STAR, THE FOOL & THE WORLD

Tarot and astrology are inextricably linked. All the cards of the Major Arcana, which comprises 22 of the Tarot's 78 cards, are 'ruled by' or connected with either one of the twelve zodiac signs, the planets and luminaries, or one of the four elements.

The 22 Major Arcana cards contain the richest symbolism of all the cards in the Tarot deck, each carrying a myriad of messages for the reader to decipher. The symbolism contained within these images represents the archetypal aspects of your character. It also describes the path your soul takes through each stage of life, revealing clues through which you can explore different parts of yourself. Each of the cards also represents an aspect of Universal human experience and has a name that either directly conveys the meaning of the card, such as Strength or Justice, or depicts individuals that represent these human archetypes, such as the Hermit or the Empress. The illustrations on each card contain one or more figures and tuning into a card's imagery enables you to grasp its meaning intuitively. Consider the demeanour of the characters, whether it is day or night, the background, any symbols, the buildings, the colours, the vegetation, the weather and the season. Every card has its own story to impart, and through entering that story you can gain deeper insights into the full picture of your journey so far, as well as illuminating your path ahead.

I have outlined three cards here for your sign: The Star, The Fool and The World, all of which have links to your zodiac sign itself Aquarius, your ruling planet Uranus, your traditional ruling planet Saturn, and your element of Air. All three cards will have special meaning for your sign, and can carry powerful messages and lessons for you to reflect upon.

★ THE STAR ★
Ruled by Aquarius

Keywords ★ Hope, Dreams, Optimism

★ KEY THEMES ★
★ Hope ★ Inspiration ★ Creativity ★ Idealism ★ Happiness ★ Good Luck ★ Rebirth ★ Renewal ★ Light After Darkness ★ The Calm After the Storm ★ Restored Hope, Faith, Inspiration and Promise ★ A Bright Future ★ Imagination ★ Faith ★ Creation ★ Good Prospects

Meditation ★ "The energy I pour into today will fuel my whole future."

Number ★ 17
Astrological Sign ★ Aquarius

The last five Major Arcana cards can be found in the heavens and, as the haiku of the Tower card reminds us, there's always hope no matter how dark the road might seem. The Star represents the idea that hope, courage and inspiration will bring the promise of better times to come.

THE STORY ★ There is peace after a storm. A star of hope and wonder shines in the heavens, promising spiritual illumination and inspiration. Below, with one foot on the land and the other poised magically on the surface of the stream of the unconscious, a near-naked maiden stands entranced, joyously receiving the waters of the pool, which rise up to her as she pours an endless shower of stars from her cupped hands. She demonstrates that as heaven nourishes the Earthly planes, the wonders of the physical world nourishes the heavens. The star in her is a star upon which to wish for pure miracles, with the guilelessness of a child. In the realm of The Star all is fresh and new, all is innocence and purity and hope. The maiden's language is poetry and art and she is in perfect accord with her spiritual gifts. The Star is a symbol of the cleansing and purification that occurs after the storm of life's upheavals calm down; it ultimately stands for the sense of wonder that heralds the new belief that dreams can come true.

THE LESSON ★ Wish upon a Star. It suggests that you should be more positive in outlook, and that while you may look to the stars for guidance, you should also make a practical effort to achieve your heart's desire. Avoid daydreaming and nurturing unattainable fantasies. The Star is a brilliant and positive influence, so take her advice and you will gain in self-confidence and travel far along life's interesting path. The Star's character is someone who hopes to achieve or tries to make their thoughts, ideas, plans or beliefs a reality. A combination of circumstances favouring your hopes and aims will ensure that your prospects are bright. So under the star-spangled sky above you, always remember that dreams *do* come true.

SYMBOLISM *★ The Star symbolises your ability you connect or reconnect with the source of life, optimism, renewal, hope and inspiration, which will propel you forward. This card follows the Tower card, and embodies the calm that comes after a hurricane, the inner peace that arises after a difficult time. It represents your ability to recapture and rediscover your dreams and to focus on bringing these dreams to fruition.

In the lady's left hand, she holds an empty jug that she is about to fill, which symbolises an awareness that energy needs to flow in both ways, and should be used to replenish the spirit as well as the material aspects. The water in the pool is the source of life. Pouring water into the pool replenishes the energy source from which the lady has drawn.

Above her, eight stars (all eight-pointed), symbolising the heavenly or higher realms, shine brightly against the backdrop of a milky night sky on the cusp of daybreak, while a bird perches on a tree in the background and a butterfly flutters overhead. The large star is the one seen by the Magistrate, while the smaller stars represent hope. The feature star emits rays of light towards the Moon and rising Sun, emphasising the subtle interconnectedness between all life and the Universe. As the maiden reaches out to touch the oneness of all life and all the Universe, the same light that radiates from the stars overhead glows from her.

The bird sitting in the Tree of Life is the ibis of immortality, a sacred bird, a symbol of the soul's ability to rise to higher levels of emotional and spiritual consciousness. It also represents a symbol of our spiritual self, waiting to drink from the wisdom-bestowing waters of the lake. The butterfly stands for transformation and resurrection. Like its animal symbols, this card comes after a crisis or 'storm', standing for light coming out of darkness, and offers peace, flow and freedom.

The Star is a good omen. A fortunate card, it indicates the hope and renewal that occurs after calamity, promising new and rich horizons, perhaps in previously unforeseen directions, but only after you have been tempered and expanded by having come through the storm. It expresses hope, a sense of healing and a return to wholeness, especially after emotional storms, for after the storm, there is peace. This card is the perfect symbol of wholeness, calm, oneness and healing. It depicts a beautiful naked maiden, sometimes depicted as Persephone of Greek legend, who spent one-third of every year with Hades, god of the Underworld, and two-thirds with her mother, the Earth goddess Demeter. She pours water from two pitchers; one flows into a pool, representing the depths of the unconscious, and the other onto dry land, representing the conscious mind. She revives the land with the water from the pool, while the morning star heralds the beginning of a new dawn, new life and new hope. In the Star we see the inner self joyfully experiencing itself. The Star is *free*.

Aquarius, the sign attributed to the Star, is the Fixed Air sign of the Water Bearer and represents the healing force in the Universe, as well as group understanding, collective sympathies, psychic sensitivities, and Universal friendship. Aquarians tend to be visionary in their outlook, and the Star prepares one for initiation, making it an effective symbolic tool for initiating oneself towards a brighter future - one that the Aquarian often envisions in his or her mind and spirit long before anyone else.

A card of enlightenment and enhanced awareness, the Star is symbolic of our faith, our belief in our hopes, and our desire that our wishes will come true, providing a sense of purpose and meaning, without which our lives become dull and lacklustre. It signifies that redemption is possible, that transformative powers are within our reach. It cleanses and releases all pain, restoring happiness and belief. The Star provides that bit of magic that spurs us on, keeping us going during times of stress or doubt. Indeed, the image of the Star reflects the inner light that can guide us through the darkness. The Star is not a card of action, but of inner calm. For the moment, the journey can wait. Destiny will unfold as it will before you. This card urges you to stay positive, for a goal is at last within your reach.

The idea of wishing upon a star is at the centre of the card's meaning, and it signifies that a wish will come true, something you have hoped for since you were a child. The wish-granting quality of the Star also shows us that the Universe is not the senseless and unjust place it often appears to be. The Star card suggests that there is always something else, even when the going is really tough. It indicates a gesture of affection, perhaps a gift, but the gifts of the Star are not always material. It symbolises insight, understanding and hope for the future, and asks that the spiritual dimension of life should not be ignored.

This card is a good indication that wishes will be fulfilled, not always in the form that one expects, but even so, the unexpected will have a good result. The Star shows good health and that gifts will be given. Some gifts may be in the form of the idea of cosmic power reaching down, blessing our Earthly life, bestowing our spirit with joy, and transmitting its healing energy.

Its main divinatory meanings are hope, faith, inspiration, bright prospects, optimism, insight, a mixing of the past and present, spiritual love, astrological influence, fulfilment and pleasure. It signifies the divine balancing of desire and work, love and expression, and hope and effort. It suggests inspiration, a deep sense of purpose, an inner knowing that things will turn out for the best, an intuitive belief in magic, and the renewal of life's force and energy. It promises and encourages imagination and a positive attitude, even when times are difficult or trying.

When you get the Star card in a reading, you know you have passed to a new level and something in you has opened to a higher plane. You are ready to ask for help, and you will receive it. A certain grace comes over you which allows you to see the future with renewed faith, and you trust in the ability of the Universe to heal you. You are ready to begin the process of transformation.

Aquarians are recommended to carry one of these cards with them to illumine their paths, and to magnetise that for which they are asking. Go forth and claim the magic which is yours by using the symbolism of The Star as your guide!

★ THE FOOL ★
Ruled by Uranus & the Element of Air

Keywords ★ Beginnings, Innocence, Exploration

★ KEY THEMES ★

"Trusting Your Inner Elf"

Fresh Beginnings ★ Adventure ★ Quest ★ Excitement ★ Asserting Your Independence ★ Creative Solutions ★ Spontaneity ★ Egolessness ★ Innocence ★ The Need For Optimism ★ Naiveté ★ Unexpected Opportunities ★ Courage ★ Folly ★ Happy-Go-Lucky Mortal, About to Step Off a Cliff into the Abyss ★ Impulse

Meditation ★ "I have the courage to step forward; I am not afraid of the unknown."

Number ★ Zero (or 22 in some decks)
Astrological Signs ★ Aquarius, Gemini, Libra & Aries

THE STORY ★ The Fool card symbolises the state of potential from which all possibilities arise. It is the purest embodiment of the self on the quest for spiritual awakening. When the Fool appears in a Tarot spread, it suggests that you are about to embark on a journey that will fundamentally change you - either literally or by changing your outlook on life. You may not be certain of what lies ahead, but you must be willing to take the chance.

THE LESSON ★ The Fool is a foolish man. And as such, he knows everything, but is unaware that he does. Or, he possesses all the gifts, all the truths, all the wisdom, all the joys, all the wonders of the seen and unseen worlds, but is totally unaware of it. He must therefore submit himself to the various trials of life to develop his faculties and become an enlightened being. The Fool represents the Self on a journey, who grows and learns with each new encounter. Wide-eyed and innocent as a newborn child, The Fool has descended from the celestial realms, eager to begin his mystical journey on the path towards enlightenment. All is new to him and he has not yet learned to fear. Living from moment to moment, going forward without plan nor care, unaware of potential perils and joyful, in his luggage he carries the memories, instincts and experiences of past lives, waiting to be utilised this time around. He carries a wand symbolising the pure faith of his actions, upon which sits a head that looks backwards, representing The Fool's past as he moves ever-forward. The dog leaping and bounding behind him symbolises the purity of the animal nature of our physical bodies and is seen in playful harmony with The Fool. The backdrop is suffused with green, the colour of growth, and the sky is filled with the fresh light of a spring season, signalling shining, new life. Like the court jesters who maintained his tradition, The Fool is truthful, and has no contaminating malice or desires.

SYMBOLISM **★ This card depicts the Fool wandering off, his few possessions slung over his shoulder in a small bag hung from a pilgrim's staff, oblivious to the chasm ahead, with his dog jumping at his leg. Symbolically, his bag carries his experiences. He does not abandon them, for he is not thoughtless, they simply do not control him in the way that *our* traumas or memories so often control our lives. The stick upon which his bag casually hangs, is, in some interpretations, actually a wand, a symbol of power and magic. The Fool card's image symbolises the instinctive life force that both holds him back and urges him on. Like its ruler Uranus, the Fool is the spirit of chaos, of the unexpected, but also about innocence and the simple joys of living. This card belongs anywhere in the deck, in combination with and between any of the other cards, offering an animating force to more static images and symbols. As such, he assists during times of transition, and also in times of difficult passage.

The Fool's staff represents the Suit of Wands, symbolic of passionate, fiery energy. He grasps the staff firmly, as he does all of life's opportunities, and although it is a symbol of power, the Fool uses it in a playful manner.

The Fool's cloak is usually blue, representing his inner search for wisdom and truth. And when he finds his enlightenment, he will be eager to communicate it to others.

The Fool is usually the first card in the Tarot deck, the starting point of the Tarot 'experience'. In some early decks he appeared at the end of the Major Arcana rather than at the beginning, as he not only begins our journey but may also accompany us throughout it - this is essentially because he symbolises our very self. When he first sets out at the beginning of his path, he is a stranger to his inner self and lives primarily in his conscious mind, but by the end of his journey he has glimpsed the deeper mysteries of his real self. The Fool seeks the truth, and turns his attention towards the spirit in search of it. There is in the Fool an element of the Divine trickster, and even though the Fool doesn't know what he is doing in the sense of logical thought, he moves from an impulse that arises out of the infinite possibilities emanating from the state represented by the number 'zero'. The Fool is simple, innocent, trusting and ignorant of the potential trials, setbacks and pitfalls that await him, and he is prepared to abandon his old ways and follow his quest by taking a leap into the unknown. Indeed, the Fool represents the need to let go of old ways and begin something new, untested and unexperienced. For those willing to follow the Fool's example and deviate from the path society has set out for us, this leap can bring joy, adventure, and finally, for those with the courage to continue even when the path becomes fearsome, the leap will bring peace, knowledge and liberation.

Containing all possibilities, the Fool represents the phenomenon of synchronicity or coincidences between happenings, and is the part of us that unconsciously connects to the greater Universal whole, so things are constantly happening to us that involve the unspoken and often unacknowledged links between our thoughts and the events outside of ourselves. If you are open to magic, you will accept these synchronicities on an intellectual level, and in turn will notice such events more frequently and learn to appreciate them more fully.

This card can be said to represent the human soul that is unselfconsciously happy to be alive, that does not yet reflect back upon itself, the spark of life that reincarnates again and again until it truly awakens to itself. Reincarnation is the secret key to the Fool, and the Fool is indeed the 'secret' key, or at least significantly the first door which opens us up to the rest of the Tarot experience. The Fool, whose awareness is limited to the present moment, moves from moment to moment, life to life, without intellectual consideration or care for what has gone before and what will be in the future. Representing innocence, the Fool is perpetually young and always starting afresh. He believes in himself and instinctively trusts his body and the general flow of life.

Astrologically, the Fool is ruled by the Air element, making it as free as the wind. Uranus, considered the most eccentric of the planets, gives the card's symbolism qualities of intellectual brilliance, intuitive flashes, lawlessness, reform, inventiveness and originality. Linked to this rebellious planet, it also promises mystery, a dash of genius, adventure, and a great opportunity to reinvent your life. It impels you to listen to your own inner guidance about following your dreams while still staying open to outside guidance and information; actively seek any insight you may need for your leap.

Although some divinatory meanings of this card are thoughtlessness, insecurity, folly, apathy, frivolity, extravagance, lack of discipline, immaturity, irrationality, hesitation, indecision, delirium, frenzy, enthusiasm and naivety, it also proclaims that nothing can harm you, whatever you do, so take a risk! It does, however, advise to look before you leap - a measured, calculated risk will reap the greatest rewards - and lessons. This card symbolises new beginnings in all senses, courageous leaps into some new phase of life, and is a particularly potent symbol when that jump is taken from some inner prompting and deep feeling rather than careful planning.

Not limited by ordinary social conventions and uncomplicated and unanalytical by nature, the Fool is never afraid to believe in something Divine or greater than ego. Naturally flowing, trusting, naïve and spontaneous, the Fool often plunges into the cosmic experience without fear or expectation. And indeed, it is the Fool in each of us which urges us away from lethargy and towards enlightenment and transformation without fear of the future.

It is also worth noting and reminding yourself that even a fool can have flashes of great wisdom and sudden lightning bolt thoughts, reminiscent of the brilliant but ever-unpredictable Uranus, this card's - and your own - mighty ruler.

★ THE WORLD/UNIVERSE ★
Ruled by Saturn & the Element of Earth

Keywords ★ Completion, Attainment, Fulfilment

★ KEY THEMES ★
★ Arrival! ★ Completion ★ Fulfilment of Hopes and Dreams ★ Crowning Achievement ★ Total Success ★ Dreams Come True ★ Expansion ★ Aspirations ★ Idealism ★ A Prize or Goal Reached ★ Acclaim ★ Graduation ★ Accomplishment ★ Attainment ★ Joy ★ Contentment ★ Gratitude ★ The Path Toward Enlightenment ★ Perfection ★ Freedom ★ A Move to the Next Level ★ Cosmic Awareness ★
Expanded Consciousness ★ Joy ★ Great Outlook ★

Number ★ 21
Astrological Signs ★ Capricorn, Taurus, Virgo & Aquarius

THE MESSAGE ★ You have arrived at the beginning of the Path to Enlightenment, or could be considerably advanced along it by now. The World card suggests a job well done - you have happily completed something of great significance. Enjoy these feelings of wholeness and completion as your amazing accomplishments have been well-earned. You're now ready to move onto something new. You have grown spiritually and have evolved to a whole new level in your understanding of the Universe and your place in it. As well as this, you have attained complete clarity, cosmic awareness, significant enlightenment, an expanded consciousness and above all, the true freedom that accompanies all this.

THE STORY ★ A statue of a woman has come to life and is dancing, looking back at a leaf she holds in her outstretched hand. Just as the Earth, Divine Mother of us all, evolved from the stars and materialised into reality, so have our physical selves been created out of the same essence so that we may dance the dance of life just as She dances through the cosmos. This dream-like journey is one of going deep within and finding our essential harmony with All There Is. When we arrive at the knowledge of who we really are we gain The World.

THE AWAKENING ★ The World is a symbol of accomplishment, of an end which is also a beginning. The journey is completed! Upon reaching the World your goal is attained and you are suffused with joy and fulfilment. Life is fully and rapturously embraced, and you are free to experience all that it offers. You realise that the end of a journey merely leads to the first step on a new one. By uniting and balancing your long-sought after inner harmony with the skills you have learned in this lifetime so far, you have achieved true success and The World can be yours. Although hard work has been required to attain this, material rewards and inner peace are promised. But overall, you must view your life in the context of the whole of life and All There Is, before you can gain the wisdom you seek. The World imparts the message that each one of us carries a world inside of us, which is neither unattainable, illusory or utopian. It is simply what we are. All the elements are gathered here so that our conscience may awaken and our future will unfold as it is meant to before us.

SYMBOLISM *★ The World card symbolises completion and renewal. It incorporates the wisdom gathered throughout the journey of the previous 21 cards. The World embodies the essence of success, arrival, fulfilment and happiness. It shows a willingness to embrace life fully and to welcome in the new.

The central figure in the World card, hermaphroditic in appearance, symbolises the integration of the masculine and feminine principles to form a complete, unified entity. The wreath is a symbol of triumph, success, rebirth and renewal, while the surrounding creatures embody different aspects of human nature.

One of the most ancient symbols of alchemy is that of Ouroboros, the dragon or serpent which lies in a circle with its tail in its mouth. This sleeping creature must be awoken for its potential to be realised, and its energies released, for us to begin - and achieve - the process of self-transformation. The circle around the dragon, a symbol without end and without beginning, symbolises the fact that one's beginning can also be found in its end, and vice versa. And so the symbol for Ouroboros never loses its meaning, for its meaning is eternity and in a sense the journey is never really completed; each ending is followed by a new beginning. Even if we eventually arrive back at the place where we first began our journey, nothing will be the same; all is transformed.

The World (or Universe), the final card of the Major Arcana, is the supreme symbol of unity and wholeness. It commonly depicts a dancing figure holding the Magician's wand and encircled by a laurel wreath. The wand is symbolic of the magic of self-transformation, while the laurel is the plant of success, victory and high achievement. The circle represents the Ouroboros (a serpent or dragon eating its own tail), a symbol of eternity. In each corner are the four Fixed signs of the zodiac: Taurus the Bull, Leo the Lion, Scorpio the Eagle and Aquarius the Man, which correspond to the four seasons of spring, summer, autumn and winter respectively, the four evangelical qualities of Man: humanity, spirituality, courage and strength, and also the four elements, which the alchemists combined to create a perfect fifth - the 'quintessence', or fifth element. This fifth element is symbolised by the central figure in the card, a genderless hermaphrodite, an image of the reconciliation of opposites, and also of balance. The card's number is twenty-one, the number of completion (three times seven, the two most magically significant numbers). The wreath may also represent zero, the symbol of infinity, with which you started the journey; therefore, the end of one journey is marking the beginning of another.

Astrologically, the World seems to be the most strongly related to the Midheaven, which is the highest point in the sky at the moment of birth. The World's divinatory meanings are completion, perfection, the rewards of labour, inner satisfaction, the end result of all your efforts, success, synthesis, fulfilment, capability, eternal life, admiration from others, ultimate change, and triumph in all your undertakings. As a symbol of completion, attainment, success and self-knowledge, she suggests that you remind yourself of what you have already achieved, and know that others are aware of you, appreciate and truly admire your past efforts. She tells you that you are now entering an extremely rewarding phase of your life when you will enjoy the benefits of all your hard work.

The World marks the end of a period of time, or the completion of a task, which has its new beginnings as a seed within. It denotes a time of celebration and the wonderful feelings that accompany any occasion during which something is finished, or made whole. It represents a deeply satisfying sense of achievement and fulfilment, suggestive of a peak experience - and expanded horizons ahead. On another level, however, any accomplishment or completion may be followed afterwards by a feeling of emptiness or deflation, as the goal has been realised and the dream made a reality. At this point, the crowned dancing figure who celebrates reaching the finishing mark, suddenly morphs again to embody a foetal-like being, waiting to re-evolve and rebirth itself as the Fool in the never-ending circular journey; in this way, The World symbolises the ending of one cycle and the commencement of another, and indeed The World represents a course that has now come full circle, and suggests you can rest on your laurels for a time before moving onto this next phase, as you have rightly earned it. You now understand your place within that system, and are ready to begin a new phase from the beginning, but this time with an elevated, higher sense of acquired wisdom, spiritual truth and inner knowing.

* Please note that the images described are not found in all Tarot decks. The images in different decks can differ considerably.

THE TAROT'S SUIT OF SWORDS ★ REPRESENTING THE AIR ELEMENT

The Swords correspond with the Air element and are an especially interesting and meaningful metaphor. Swords, or the mind, organise by dividing, and quite literally cutting through things. Being of the Air element, the Swords are associated with ideas, the intellect, mental activity, thought processes, and mental insights, attitudes and clarity. Air cannot be seen, gripped, grasped or commanded of, and can only be felt with subtle 'other' senses - the higher mind being one of them. We know the air is there through its apparent physical presence such as wisps of wind, but we cannot see it, touch it or even embrace it. In this way, the Swords suit can signify a certain elusiveness, something that can somehow evade us. But it is nonetheless a powerful force. With the Air suit, illusions are recognised and shattered in the pursuit of the inner kernel of truth, knowledge and wisdom that the Swords embody - but the quest is fraught with painful lessons and is not always easy. These challenges will lead to greater understanding. The story of Swords begins with the core connection to the all-wise, all-seeing eye of the spirit. This Divine essence first manifests itself in the mind and then those thoughts create form. Everything you see results from an initial thought that was put into action. As well as relating to the conscious direction of the intellect and will, the Swords also reveal hidden motivations and attitudes that can influence a situation. Cards from this suit advise us to either go to the core of the problem or to cut ourselves free in order to start afresh.

Considered to be powerful and potentially destructive and dangerous, the Tarot Swords can indicate battles and enemies, but they can also be used constructively, to summon courage and a more conscious and astute quality of mind. Even though they have long had a reputation as harbingers of unhappiness and discomfort, this suit still serves a useful purpose. Without the ability to use reason and logic we risk being constantly swept away by our emotions, with all the potential for disaster that this could bring. The Swords can therefore assist in bringing about increased clarity and foresight, which we can use to avert trouble that may be brewing, and nip explosiveness in the bud. The Swords may be connected with hostility, sorrows, loss, struggle, action, change, bitterness, power, oppression, malice and conflict, but they are also associated with fortitude, decisiveness, audacity, tact, fairness, strength, bravery, ambition, force and truth, as well as with ideas and communication. Swords are almost always double-edged, which symbolises the fine balance that is needed between the intellect and power, and how these two forces can be used for good or evil. Overall, the Suit of Swords reveals our state of mind and how we use its mighty force. In a deck of playing cards, Swords correspond to Spades.

THE LUCKY 13 ★ AQUARIAN TIPS FOR INCREASED MAGIC, LUCK & MAGNETISM

1 ★ Incorporate Aquarian symbols into your daily life to remind yourself of your soul's mission.

2 ★ Use the crystal Amethyst in any form in your daily life - wear it, meditate with it, hold it and carry it with you everywhere! Amethyst is the stone of the Third Eye, spirituality and psychic awareness. It brings calm, peace, inspiration and balance, all of which are emotions or states of being that assist in attracting wonderful things to you.

3 ★ Wear or surround yourself with the colour electric blue and the stone or the colour turquoise. Turquoise is the stone of friendship, and so aligns with the Eleventh House, which is the astrological house ruled by Aquarius. It also brings hope, discovery, peace and balance, all of which are emotions or states of being that assist in attracting wonderful things to you.

4 ★ Learn the way of the Lion by learning courage, boldness and confidence. Leo has much to teach the Aquarian soul. Roar … Wear the crown … Seat yourself at the head of the Table of Life … Feel the wonders of the plains under your feet … Enjoy the feasts and fruits of your journey … Lead the pride … Sit atop the Mighty Throne… it's all within you!

5 ★ Use your lucky numbers 4, 5 and 8, whenever you are needing an extra stroke of luck.

6 ★ Magnify and celebrate your originality, quirks, eccentricities, uniqueness and inventiveness.

7 ★ Remind yourself of your mission constantly, that is by speaking, breathing and *truly living* your brilliant ideas and insights - bring them out into the sunshine!

8 ★ Focus your energies on exploring your inner genius and transforming yourself through your higher thinking faculties - which are strongly accessible to the acutely intellectually-sensitive Aquarian mind.

9 ★ Use your innate power of magnetism and futuristic thinking to visualise and draw that which you desire towards you.

10 ★ Tap into and utilise your ability to guide, heal and transform others through sharing your mind and thoughts. Connect with your brilliant ideas through any means possible. But to do that, you'll need to come down from that lonely mountaintop from time to time. We need you down here!

11 ★ View your eccentric nature as a strength and call forth the powers of your unusual, gifted, unique self. Be who you really are and the rest will fall into place.

12 ★ Become the 'Original Genius/Inventor' that you were born to be!

13 ★ Once you have mastered true self-confidence, courage and boldness, learn to share the resulting abundance, insights and knowledge with others so they too can walk the Higher Path!

HAVE YOU PACKED YOUR MAGICAL BAG FOR THE JOURNEY?

If you wish to increase and draw more luck, love and abundance into your life, a power pack is essential. For Aquarians, I would recommend carrying or wearing the following items on you on your travels. Then just sit back and watch as magic pours into your experiences and realities, both inner and outer!

★ One of each of the following gemstones: Turquoise, Garnet, Aquamarine, Amethyst, Zircon
★ Tarot cards The Star and The Fool (and The World/Universe card too, if you wish)
★ An otter in any form (use your imagination!)
★ Something made of lead
★ A key symbol in any form
★ A postcard or image from a tropical place (representing your Sanguine disposition). Bon Voyage!
★ A postcard from the future to yourself, proclaiming, 'Wish You Were Here!'

A FINAL WORD ★ TAPPING INTO THE MAGIC OF AQUARIUS

There is something inherently magical about Aquarius, the Water Bearer. Blessed with a lack of arrogance, a brilliant mind and dazzling foresight, they truly are the Magical Future-Dwellers of the zodiac, affecting everyone around them with their power and sense of the weird and wonderful. Never malicious but ever perversely contradictory and rebellious, the Aquarian soul wants to connect with other like-minded souls. To really tap into your true magic, this mind and soul connection with kindred spirits is imperative to your life's spring of wellbeing. You are the sign of the group leader. Connect! Exchange! Brainstorm! Share! Embrace! Love! Shine!

Inside anyone who has a strong Aquarius influence in their natal chart, is someone who is deeply uncertain of their identity. The typical Aquarian possesses a powerful and magnetic intellect, but your ego is said to be the weakest and most precarious of the zodiac; you are not a proficient self-promoter and generally shy away from attention and focus. Although perversely reluctant to share your sparkling ideas, talent and futuristic prophecies, Aquarius is often under-credited and is actually the most intellectual of the signs; underneath a cool façade, you are pure genius just bursting with mind-blowing ideas that need to be brought out to air! They're no use sitting in the dusty recesses of your mind ... or off wildly living it up on some other planet.

Further, like your ruling planet Uranus, you are the Divine Rebel of the zodiac, and although this can pay dividends in the form of societal change, you need to build within yourself a strong centre that you can return to in order to rest and refresh. Aquarius rules the circulatory system, and while this assists in the movement of your thoughts, you also need that strong centre to fall back on; for this, you would do well to take lessons in *heart* from your opposite sign, Leo, and its rulership over the heart, the life force, the core, *the centre*. Your mind and nervous system usually rule you, rather than the other way around. In order to master yourself, you need to put yourself in a position to manifest on the Earthly plane that which you visualise by becoming one with the source of your mind. This means you have to find a way to observe your own prodigious thinking processes and not just *be* your thoughts - by keeping them cooped up and creating nervous system and minor mental health disturbances in the process, which is at the root of your suffering.

There is tremendous creative and visionary potential inherent in Aquarius, but you are also fixed and tenacious, meaning that may have difficulties giving up old opinions, ideas and positions that should've been left behind long ago. While you're busy living in the future, the ideas of your past may be stuck on that stick in the stream. Unpack your baggage from time to time, Aquarius, the journey is a lot lighter without it!

Ultimately, your sign represents freedom, especially the kind of freedom which comes from transcending the body and Earthly life, freedom of thought, the power of individuality harnessed to serve the greater whole, and importantly (to Aquarians at least) the union of science and magic. Aquarians are big believers in magic, despite everything their logical left brain has 'taught' them. Not only can they get completely lost in Wonderland, they believe wholeheartedly in the adage, "When in Rome (or Wonderland) …" - they just do it a little differently to the Wonderlandians in order to stand out - and will live by this motto their entire lives. Which isn't a bad thing at all. The world needs more souls of your ilk, who stand apart from the herd. Great things transpire from those who dare to be different and above all, from those who dare to dream.

Finally, to attune yourself to luck, harmony and success, Aquarians should wear, eat, inhale, meditate upon, create, design, and dance with any or all of the suggested luck-enhancers for your Sun sign to receive the most beneficial astral vibrations these 'boosters' can offer you. Wearing, decorating and working with the amazing powers of all your lucky guides, animals, crystals, woods, colours, cards, herbs, foods, places, talismans, planetary influences, charms, numbers, and other magical tips contained within the words of this very book, will bring you greater abundance, love, magic, energy, happiness and personal power, and attract all manner of things to you like bees to sweet flowers. This, my fellow Aquarian friends, I promise you - and Aquarians *never* lie.

> Good luck on the rest of your amazing life journey, and may the LUCK be with you!

Lani is also available for personal Astrology, Numerology, Aura * & Tarot reading consultations, via post, email, Skype and in-person. Please email lalana76@bigpond.com for more information.

* In-person only

Facebook Page ★ Astrology Magic

Other Books in the **Lucky Astrology** Series

Lucky Astrology ★ Aries
Lucky Astrology ★ Taurus
Lucky Astrology ★ Gemini
Lucky Astrology ★ Cancer
Lucky Astrology ★ Leo
Lucky Astrology★ Virgo
Lucky Astrology ★ Libra
Lucky Astrology ★ Scorpio
Lucky Astrology ★ Sagittarius
Lucky Astrology ★ Capricorn
Lucky Astrology ★ Pisces

Order your copies now, from White Light Publishing House, at www.whitelightpublishingau.com

www.ingramcontent.com/pod-product-compliance
Lightning Source LLC
Chambersburg PA
CBHW071155300426
44113CB00009B/1223